*"If any of you lacks wisdom, let him ask
God, who gives generously to all without
reproach, and it will be given him."*

JAMES 1:5

DEVOTIONAL FOR THOSE
COPING WITH TRAGEDY

A JOURNEY BACK
TO GOD

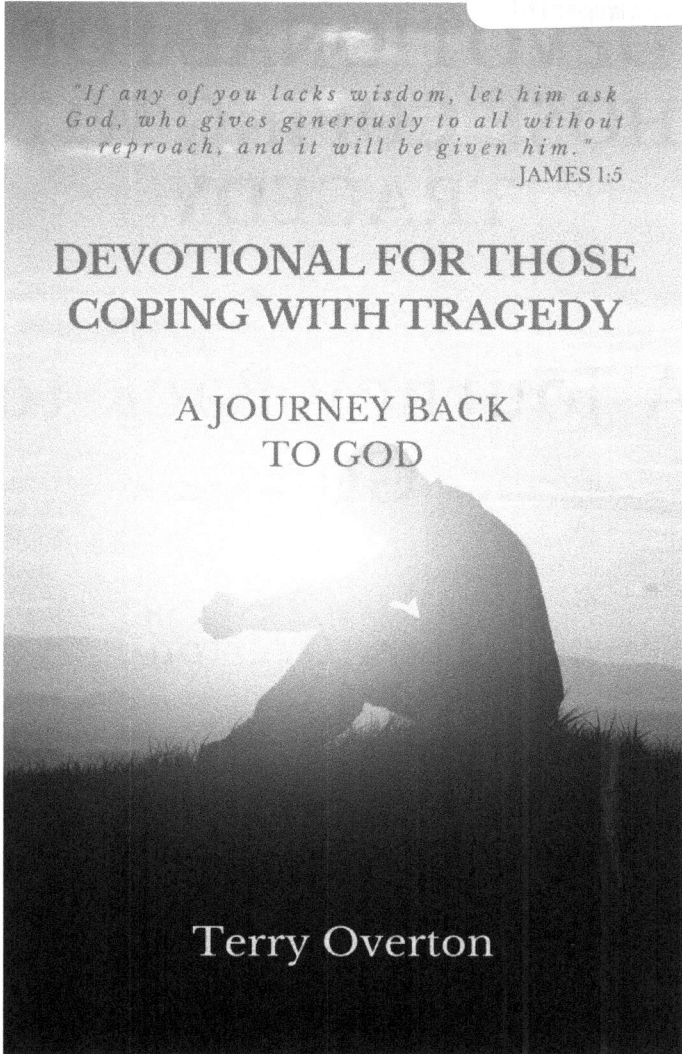

Terry Overton

DEVOTIONAL FOR THOSE COPING WITH TRAGEDY

A Journey Back to God

Terry Overton

Christian Publishing House

Cambridge, Ohio

Christian Publishing House

Professional Conservative Christian

Publishing of the Good News!

CPH Since 2005

Unless otherwise indicated, Scripture quotations are from the English Standard Version (ESV)

The Holy Bible, English Standard Version. ESV® Text Edition: 2016. Copyright © 2001 by Crossway Bibles, a publishing ministry of Good News Publishers.

DEVOTIONAL FOR THOSE COPING WITH TRAGEDY: A Journey Back to God

Authored by Terry Overton

This is a work of fiction. Names, locations, characters, and incidents are the product of the author's imagination.

ISBN-13: **978-1-945757-92-1**

ISBN-10: **1-945757-92-2**

Dear Readers:

I have been where you are. Many years ago, my family suffered a very personal trauma. My initial reaction was to be angry with God. To denounce Him. To reject Him. I traveled a long journey that included moves from one city to another, moves from one job to another, and many other failed solutions or "fixes" in my personal life, as I searched for happiness again. I experienced sadness, depression, and anxiety. My journey back to God took many years. I returned to God as quickly as I could. I traveled the journey He planned for me to take. I could not have reached Him any other way. He knew that. He continued loving me all the while.

If you scoured the research on the internet or other sources trying to make sense of your experiences, you might have found that "experts" will say the adjustment or healing after trauma may require 4 to a dozen steps. In reality, many of these sources include little if any of the experience of anger with God and peace again with your relationship with Him. Although as a professional, I read many of those articles about trauma victims, they did not seem to fit what I felt.

Finally coming back to Him and feeling peacefulness about the trauma and the consistent love from God, my next step on my journey was to provide the Christian perspective to others by writing this book. Had I found a book such as this during my trials, I might have understood more quickly, I might not have felt so alone, I might have moved back to God more quickly. This book follows the sequence that I traveled on my own journey (See Appendix 2 for the sequence of my own journey). Your journey may be different, but you may find some common feelings and experiences within this book.

My prayers are with you. Your pain is real. Your sadness is deep. Your heart is broken. You feel as if no one else can truly understand. If this describes you, if you are struggling with trauma, a tragedy, or painful events in your life, please take a few moments each day to read this book, consult your Bible, and when you are ready, pray. When you are ready, talk to God. God is waiting for you. Know that He loves you even if you have a hard time loving Him at the moment.

Before you begin this book, turn to Appendix 1 and take the self-assessment. This will give you an idea of where you might be in your own faith journey.

Blessings to you,

Terry Overton

Table of Contents

Life Before

This devotional book begins at the beginning before the tragedy. This is the starting point for you, too. Because your life before the trauma was what you considered "normal," we will start there and move through the process to the other side of the trauma, through the journey all the way to the end, seeking peace again and finding God.

Before the Tragedy or Trauma-Assess Your Foundation

Think about your life before the tragedy. If you have not already completed the Self-Assessment in Appendix 1, please do so at this time.

"Delight yourself in the Lord, and he will give you the desires of your heart" Psalm 37: 4.

Traumas include any number of events that happen tragically to individuals and their families. A trauma or tragedy could be a catastrophic event, such as a flood, fire, or storm that destroys your home or results in death or injury. It could be that someone committed a crime against you, violated you, a family member or, your property, or it could be a personal relationship trauma such as a divorce, separation, or death of family member. Terminal illnesses, accidents, miscarriages, or chronic disease or injury of you or a family member are also tragic. It may be a one-time event, or it may be a repeated or ongoing.

Think back to the time before that traumatic event had happened in your life. You may have been living your dream life with a happy family, terrific job, stable income, and faith in God. It is important, as you look back, to understand that you were meant to be there at that time, with a peaceful existence. Your peaceful existence likely prepared you for what was about to happen. You probably had already developed a support group of family, friends, spouse, or others. These may be the same people you will call on later, as you work through this trauma.

God places us where we need to be. We may not understand why we are where we are at the time of the event, and we may never understand why a trauma had to happen. During a trauma, it is hard to remember that you are not alone. You may <u>feel</u> completely alone. You may feel that no one else could possibly understand. But know this: **God is with you**. Family members and friends are with you. So now, look back to the time before the trauma and ask yourself, why did God give me those blessings of peaceful life and family before the trauma? Before the trials? He knew you would need them. Remember those people are your supports. They may not be able to know what it is like in your shoes, but they know you are hurting and they want to help you with your pain. Somehow in the tapestry of life, God will weave the trauma into something meaningful later.

> *"Therefore, since we have been justified by faith, we have peace with God through our Lord Jesus Christ. Through him we have also obtained access by faith into this grace in which we stand, and we rejoice in the hope of the glory of God. More than that, we rejoice in our sufferings, knowing that suffering produces endurance, and endurance produces character, and character produces hope, and hope does not put us to shame, because God's love has been poured into our hearts through the Holy Spirit who has been given to us." Romans 5: 1-5*

Prayers will be suggested at the end of each devotional. It may be difficult at first to pray. If you can, take a moment to quiet your heart and say the prayer that follows.

Heavenly Father, I have been blessed in my life. Even in the mist of these events, please help me to recognize my blessings. Amen.

Trauma or Event Part 1

Think about the events and how your world seems different now. The tragedy may be difficult to acknowledge at first. You may have trouble believing the event happened.

> *"Beloved, do not be surprised at the fiery trial when it comes upon you to test you, as though something strange were happening to you." 1 Peter 4:12*

The trauma happened. You may have witnessed the trauma. It may have happened directly to you, or you may have heard a family member disclose the details of the trauma or tragedy. You may have heard the news of the traumatic event from a police officer or a doctor. Whatever the event, you were not prepared. You had no say so in the occurrence of the event or in how the messenger delivered the news. You had no say so in the timing or place of the event. But it happened.

If the event happened directly to you, you might replay the event over and over in your mind. Little things may trigger the memory, and the sequence of events happens again in your mind. It may be triggered when you hear a certain sound, smell a particular smell, or return to a specific place. You may not be able to stop thinking about it.

If someone first told you about the event, you may hear those words over and over. You may have lashed out at the deliverer of the message, telling the messenger it can't be true. There must be a mistake. You may not be able to control your initial reaction.

The verse above, written by Peter, was written for the early Christians who were being persecuted. Many died. Many were tortured. Many suffered traumas. We can look to Peter's words to help us make sense out of our initial feelings about the trauma. As stated in the verse above, what happened to you feels strange. You feel that you are thrown directly into the fire. You have been thrown into a dungeon or a cave of despair. Your world feels completely out of control, or you can't stop crying or shaking, as if your own body is completely out of your control. Your heart may race, your stomach may be upset, you may not feel like eating or sleeping at the time of the trauma. You may not sleep for the nights immediately following the traumatic event. These feelings are not unusual and certainly are understandable under the circumstances.

Whatever the news or trauma, you feel that your life has changed forever. It has. You may not be able to think about anything else but know this: **you will make it to the other side of the trauma.** You will make it through this because God is a God of love and salvation and will be with you. Also, know that you are on His time clock, so the event that just happened is likely just the beginning of a journey. That's ok. All is as it should be. The journey may last days, or, it may last years. You are on the journey you need to be on to return back to God. Do not expect to move through this any faster than you are right now. Do not feel that you should "be over it." Do not worry that others tell you should move on. You move as you can. God will help you. God's hand is always outstretched, reaching for you, when you are ready, He will be there. He is a loving God, and He continues to love you always.

The verse below was one that was written by Jeremiah as he lamented about the destruction of the city he loved, Jerusalem. He began to follow God more closely following this great loss and prayed as he hoped that his city would be restored. As he noted, it is important to wait quietly or pray and be closer to God as you wait for salvation. For the sufferer of trauma, it takes time and patience to make the journey back to a more normal life. During this time period, you can pray that you will be able to walk closer to God.

"It is good that one should wait quietly for the salvation of the Lord" Lamentations 3:26

Heavenly Father, I need your help each day. I may have difficulty thinking about what has happened. Please give me strength. Amen.

Trauma or Event Part 2

Does this event seem like it is the most significant event that has happened to you? Are you able to think about this event as a test of your faith? Remember that God loves you.

"Do not fear what you are about to suffer. Behold, the devil is about to throw some of you into prison, that you may be tested..." Revelation 2:10

The verse from Revelation was written to warn people that we will be tested for our faith. John wrote this chapter of Revelation as a letter to churches of that time warning the members to stay strong in their faith and to not give in to the temptation to fall away from their faith. He wanted Christians to stand firm in their beliefs of God and Jesus.

There is no doubt that we all have trials. But the one you suffered is different. This one changed your life and perhaps the lives of others around you. This trauma came without warning. It caught you off guard. This is a test like you have never experienced before. The verse above tells you not to fear what you are about to suffer. Since you may have had no warning of the trauma or tragedy, or of its severity, perhaps you did not experience fear before the trauma. You may experience fear or anxiety afterward. Or you may not feel anything at all. You may feel numb. Any and all of these reactions are not uncommon.

Because it is a severe test, different than others you have had in your life, you react differently. One reaction you likely have not experienced prior to this event, but may experience at this time, is the rejection of God.

You may begin to feel that God cannot possibly exist, because if God existed, this event would not have occurred. You wonder how you could have ever believed in God. You may have dismissed things that used to be important to you. This can include dismissing everyday things you used to do, simple things. You may not care about much at all, even your appearance or eating or sleeping. You may change socially. Maybe you have stopped talking to your friends or family. Maybe you don't even answer your phone.

Remember, this event is testing your faith. This may be the most significant test of your life. As you begin to move through this test, you might first need a moment. You need time and space. That is understandable. Take a deep breath. Spend time with yourself gathering your thoughts. This might mean a few days off from work, or time spent alone or with family members. This is a test, but know this: **today is the beginning of the journey**. You may need to rest before the journey begins. God will be waiting.

"And when the Lord saw her, he had compassion on her and said to her, 'Do not weep'" Luke 7:13

The verse from Luke is telling of an event that happened when Jesus was walking toward a town gate. He noticed a woman who was mourning the loss of her child. He felt such compassion for her and told her not to weep. Jesus felt compassion for all mankind because He was also a human. We feel sorrow and empathy for each other. Be strong. Thank God for the gift of compassion we share with each other and with Jesus.

Heavenly Father, thank you for giving us the gift of compassion for others. Thank you for caring about each of our sorrows. Amen.

Overwhelming Feelings of Disbelief

A common first reaction to a trauma or news of a traumatic event happening to a loved one is complete disbelief or even denial that the event happened or is happening. This phase of denial may be necessary for you. This may help you process the event when you are ready.

"Be still, and know that I am God..." Psalm 46:10

An initial reaction of complete disbelief is a way that humans react to shocking news or tragic events. If someone relayed the message to you, about the accident, the diagnosis, the crime, the trauma, you might think that person is mistaken. It is not true. They have their facts wrong. It did not happen like they think it happened.

You may desperately search for someone to provide a different story. You feel the need to talk to another police officer who will say it was not your child at the scene or they did not witness the event in the same way. You might think you need to talk to another doctor pursuing a different diagnosis or locate a different specialist who can give you or your loved one another type of medical test for a better diagnosis. You may tell yourself the abuse you thought you suffered last night was not "that bad." You may try to tell yourself the rape you experienced was probably "encouraged" by your own behavior. These are defenses against knowing the truth. But as you go through this searching, you realize, it did happen exactly as you thought or as you were told. It is true. It cannot be denied.

Once the event has been confirmed, you experienced shock or even a shut-down. You may feel robotic in your day-to-day functioning. You go through the methodical motions of driving your loved one to their medical treatments, taking your child to their therapist, or even the mechanical motions of getting dressed to go to work. You may feel numb or dead on the inside. It feels surreal. It may feel like you are functioning in an alternate reality.

Why? Because your world has changed. And you are now transitioning to the "new normal." But this will be a temporary stop on your journey. Know this: **You will not linger here.**

You may also want the process to move more quickly. You might be demanding answers or solutions immediately that cannot be provided to you. Resolving the trauma will take time.

> *"For still the vision awaits its appointed time; it hastens to the end-it will not lie. If it seems slow, wait for it; it will surely come; it will not delay" Habakkuk 2:3*

The verse above is an answer to Habakkuk from God. This prophet had asked God why is it that bad or evil people seem to get away with unjust actions? He wanted God to act. He was tired of seeing the same bad things happen day after day. God responded that justice will come and that Habakkuk would need to be patient.

You will find yourself moving on. In the meantime, keep functioning in your day-to-day routines. Keep talking with family or friends who know you are hurting. If you feel that your pain is insufferable, and you cannot make it, you should reach out to someone during this time. A friend, a fellow Christian, a neighbor, a pastor, a family member, a counselor, will be there for you.

Heavenly Father, I know you help those who need you. My spirit is crushed. Please help me to find peace. Amen.

Rejection of God-Part 1

Because your world has turned upside down, you cannot understand what has happened. The world makes no sense and therefore, God makes no sense.

"The fool says in his heart, 'there is no God.'" Psalm 14:1

Whether you were a regular church-going person before the trauma, a devout Christian, someone who believed in God, or someone who never believed in God, one common reaction after the trauma is to reject or denounce God. You feel that there can be no God at all because this trauma is evidence of that. A loving God would not allow this trauma to happen. A loving God would not allow evil to be in the world. A loving God would not allow cancer, miscarriages, divorce, child abuse, substance abuse, sexual abuse, spousal abuse, rape, car accidents, the death of a loved one, or any other traumatic event. A loving God would never allow your child to be arrested, or allow your child to commit a crime, or for your child to get a terminal disease.[1]

You may shout at God, shake your fist, or just tell Him in your own private thoughts that you no longer believe. If you were not a believer before, you say "See, I knew there was no God." Others encourage your faith, suggesting you pray, and you tell them you do not believe in God anymore. You may tell God you are angry. But He is not angry with you. He loves you always.

If you were a devout believer before, you might feel that all of your prayers, your good works, your offerings, your church attendance, your volunteering to help others, all were for naught. God abandoned you when you needed Him. He was not there for

---

[1] Why has God Permitted Wickedness and Suffering?
http://bit.ly/2qHkwYR
Why is Life So Unfair?
http://bit.ly/2p43Ai9
Does God Step in and Solve Our Every Problem Because We are Faithful?
http://bit.ly/2qLdxgN

you. It is not unusual for those who were devout in their faith to fall away from God. If you were a regular church going person, you may begin slipping away from the church or stop attending altogether.

Recognize that all of these feelings are not uncommon. You are not the first person to feel this way. You will not be the last. This may indeed be something that God expects you to go through before you can reach the final destination of your journey. This may actually be a requirement before you begin your journey. This may be the only way for you to begin, by starting completely over with your faith. Know this: **Sometimes a heart must be broken so the Holy Spirit can work its way back in.** During this time, God still loves you and is waiting.

"It is good for me that I was afflicted, that I might learn your statutes" Psalm 119:71

"Jesus answered him, "What I am doing you do not understand now, but afterward you will understand" John 13:7.

The verse from John was a reply from Jesus to the disciple, Simon Peter. Jesus was about to wash the feet of his disciples. By his response, we see that, like the act of washing feet, Jesus often does things we cannot understand until later. The way you are going through this event may make more sense to you further down the faith journey. God knows the full picture and will be there for you always.

Heavenly Father, thank you for your patience. Help me to accept your guidance and your strength. Amen.

Rejection of God-Part 2

As long as rejection of God remains in your heart and mind, this negative feeling will linger in the background of all other things happening in your day-to-day life.

"Wait for the Lord; be strong, and let your heart take courage; wait for the Lord!" Psalm 27:14

It is common that people suffering from traumas feel angry and reject God for a period of time. Your anger and rejection of God may spill over into anger and rejection of all things that are good. You may reject anyone having anything to do with the past traumatic events. You may reject others trying to help you. You may snap at others or make angry comments.

You may reject any form of help. This includes guidance from the Bible, church, counselors, friends, family, and even acquaintances trying to offer you help in your time of need.

You feel this trauma was unjust. It was not fair. It was not right. If a crime was committed against you, it was a sin. It was uncalled for evil. Whatever the event, you are angry that it happened. You are angry because you feel it did not need to happen. You are angry because this event or disease rarely happens at all so, why did it happen to you or your loved one? You lash out. You may have angry outbursts more days than not. You feel incensed inside. You may hold a grudge. You may speak angrily to or about others.

In this mindset of anger, all other things seem insignificant. Your day-to-day concerns no longer have meaning or importance for you. Blessings are for other people. Every day matters are for others who have not known this trauma.

"Be sober-minded; be watchful. Your adversary the devil prowls around like a roaring lion, seeking someone to devour" 1 Peter 5:8

Many people in similar circumstances feel the same way. The anger. The unhappiness. The rage. These feelings are indications that you need more time. You may need more space. God is waiting. He is giving you a wide berth on this journey. He may not nudge you yet. He may be standing right beside you, watching and waiting. But know this: **He is there**. He is being patient. He knows the pain you are experiencing. He is allowing you more time before you begin the journey. Soon, He will be walking beside you rather than standing beside you. He will be *walking* beside you because you will be walking the first few steps on your own journey.

If you are already a Christian, you may have forgotten that, if you were baptized, even if you are angry and not speaking to God, you may feel the Holy Spirit lingering within your heart. The Spirit is waiting for the opportunity. When will that opportunity happen? God knows when you are ready. At that time, you will begin.

"And I will give you a new heart, and a new spirit I will put within you. And I will remove the heart of stone from your flesh and give you a heart of flesh". Ezekiel 36:26

The verse from Ezekiel was a promise made by God that He would give a new heart to save the people of Israel. We now know that the new heart of flesh He promised those many years ago was Jesus and the Holy Spirit. We too have that love within our hearts. Suffering trauma may mean you will require a little extra time to return to your faith and feel the love in your heart.

Heavenly Father, thank you for giving us your Son. Help me to renew my spirit and feel love again in my heart. Amen.

A Quick Fix

Tragedy causes unrest within our minds. We tend to think we can control our worlds. We cannot. So, we try to "fix things."

"Many are the plans in the mind of a man, but it is the purpose of the Lord that will stand" Proverbs 19:21

An initial reaction to the trauma is to do something, to do anything. This is how we are made. After trauma, it would just make everything better if we could do something if we could fix things. Why do we have this need? It would make us feel like we are in control of our life again.

When trauma or a traumatic event occurs, it is out of your control. You certainly would not have willed the event to happen. In fact, if you could have controlled it, that would have been the last thing you would ever have happen. But it was not in your control. And now, to help you regain control of your life, you want to do something. You may also believe taking some kind of action may lessen the pain.

What might that look like? You arrange a trip to get away from it all. You move to another neighborhood or another city. You change jobs, sell your house, remarry right away. Anything to make you feel that you can control your own world. Anything to keep you from facing the pain. Anything that might help make the pain go away.

These plans might give you more space and time. These types of quick fixes might help you to get your mind off of the trauma or serve as a diversion away from the event. And sometimes, these plans or activities are actually therapeutic. But what happens next?

When you return home from that trip away, you are faced with the same environment or event. The traumatic event reminders remain. If you moved or changed jobs, marriages, or other life circumstances, then you will find yourself realizing, the trauma or event is still in your mind. You have not made progress on your journey at all. You may not have inched any closer to God and peacefulness. But, once you realize that your plans did not help you deal with the event, you might be back at square one. Only this time, you might understand that the journey you needed to make wasn't to the airport, abroad, a new house, a new city, or a new job. The journey you need to start is the one back to God. You may still have many, many miles to go. That is perfectly ok. It may take much more time than your move to a new city or job. But now you realize that there are other things you need to do in order to move to the peaceful life you want.

Please know that moving forward does not require you ever to accept what happened as "ok." It will never be ok that your house was destroyed, your love one died, your child was traumatized. It will never be all right. But know this: **you can move forward.** You will not be stuck in the same place forever.

"And my God will supply every need of yours according to his riches in glory in Christ Jesus" Philippians 4:19

Paul wrote a letter to the new believers in Philippi with information about how we should live as Christians. He tells the new Christians that God will meet their needs as they continue their work in growing their faith. For those who have suffered trauma, God will provide for you too. He will guide you and be by your side as you continue your journey.

Heavenly Father, please help me to know that you know all of my needs. Help me to remember that you are by my side even through this difficult time. Amen.

Depression and Sadness-Part 1

The realization that our world has changed, and we are stuck with what happened, causes a sensation of helplessness in our own lives. This changes our outlook on life.

"A man's spirit will endure sickness, but a crushed spirit who can bear?" Proverbs 18:14

"The Lord is near to the brokenhearted and saves the crushed in spirit." Psalm 34:18

Whether you attempted a quick fix or remained at home in the same environment and same circumstances, the next stage of your journey may be feelings of depression, loneliness, anxiousness, or sadness. These feelings may be pervasive, and you may feel like this every day, or more days than not, especially in the beginning. If these feelings do not allow you to eat or sleep, or if you are feeling that there is no future, contact a counselor or pastor immediately.[2]

This phase of your journey may be the longest phase. Do not be surprised by this. Do not feel that something is wrong with you because you are in this phase for an extended time period. It may be part of the process. Even though it may last a while, it will not last forever. You will move forward although it may be slow at first.

So, why are you so sad? Anxious? Depressed? Your world changed. It changed significantly. You could not control what happened. In truth, nobody can control everything that happens in life. You might be able to make decisions about aspects of your life,

---

[2] Dealing with Our Depression (http://tiny.cc/fa9bty) How Can You Deal With Anxiety? (http://tiny.cc/098bty) Your Feelings Don't Have to Control You (http://tiny.cc/cm97sy) Satan's Battle for the Christian Mind (http://tiny.cc/1vl8sy) (Spiritual Sicknesses of Mind and Heart (http://tiny.cc/8xl8sy) Get the Correct Mental Grasp (http://tiny.cc/31l8sy) Dealing with Destructive Self-Defeating Thoughts (http://tiny.cc/s4l8sy) What Is the Mind of Christ? (http://tiny.cc/v5l8sy) Christians Must Be Sound in Mind (http://tiny.cc/g6l8sy) Be Transformed by the Renewal of Your Mind (http://tiny.cc/q7l8sy) Keeping the Mind Renewed (http://tiny.cc/e8l8sy) No Longer Walk in the Futility of the Old Mind (http://tiny.cc/zh97sy) The Power of Prayer (http://tiny.cc/jzl8sy) Why Does God Reject Some Prayers (http://tiny.cc/f0l8sy) How Can We Improve Our Prayers? (http://tiny.cc/z0l8sy)

but other things are not in our control. It still does not seem fair or just that this event happened. But it happened. Things are no longer as they were before the event. But there will be a peaceful future.

During this phase, what can you do to feel better? Remember the blessings or good things you have in your life now and in the past. If you lost a loved one, remember their blessing in your life. If a loved one has a traumatic health event, be thankful you can be of service to them.

If a traumatic event happened to you, it might be hard to get the traumatic event out of your mind long enough to think about these positive thoughts. It may feel impossible at first, but give it a try now and then. There is no rush. But try some simple steps. Go outside, breathe the fresh air, look up, and look around you. There are some amazing things happening right outside your door. The sun rises and sets, birds sing, the wind blows the clouds by your view. Rain happens, storms occur, the sun bursts through, or a rainbow shoots across the sky. Just pause on the journey and observe the handiwork of God.

Allow yourself time to think about the past. And then allow yourself time to think about the future. At first, you may spend more time thinking about the past but gradually think about other things.

Where are you on your journey? You are taking a step. You are taking a step forward to the future. There may be days that you find you cannot move further or you may even take a step back once in a while. But you are moving. Getting over any trauma may take a long time. Do not punish yourself by thinking you should be over it. Know this: **God will take you through the journey at the speed you need in order to reach the final outcome.**

"Answer me quickly, O Lord! My spirit fails! Hide not your face from me, lest I be like those who go down to the pit." Psalm 143:7

"You hold my eyelids open; I am so troubled that I cannot speak" Psalm 77:4

Heavenly Father, my heart is hurting, and I ask for your help. Please give me the strength to know the blessings you have given

me and help me to think more about those wonderful blessings. Amen[3]

---

[3] Dealing with Our Depression
http://tiny.cc/p722sy

Depression and Sadness-Part 2

The feelings of sadness and depression may color your days for an extended period of time. This does not mean you will always feel this way. Remember that God loves you even though you may not feel it right now.

"Likewise the Spirit helps us in our weakness. For we do not know what to pray for as we ought, but the Spirit himself intercedes for us with groanings too deep for words" Romans 8:26

During these days of deep sadness, God is still waiting for you. As the verse states above, the Holy Spirit will help you in your weakness. You may not be ready yet to pray. But God will know what you need. If your sadness is very deep and you are unable to sleep or eat, you should contact your pastor, counselor, or friend. You will be heard and understood and supported. You may need to just be with someone, a companion, to share a meal, watch a movie, or just go for a walk. No talking is really required, but be with someone in your deepest sorrow. Others may reach out to you. When they do, remember they are doing what is needed, what God knows you need. Let them. You may also be filling a need they have to be with you. Allow them this honor so that they may also serve you in this way and thereby, serve God.

"Therefore encourage one another and build one another up, just as you are doing" 1 Thessalonians 5:11

"Truly I say to you, as you did it to one of the least of these my brothers, you did it to me," Matthew 25:40

As the Scripture says, others are to build you up, and later, when you are ready, you may wish to support others. But for now, allow others to be with you. The verse from Matthew is one spoken by Christ who said that by serving each other, you are also providing a service for Christ. In this way, your family and friends are not only assisting you; they are providing a service that Christ expects of all Christians. Even though you may not be too sure about spending time with others, allow your friends and family to be with you because they want to do so.

God's knowledge of what you need extends beyond others helping or supporting you. God will help you to understand that there is a future, there will be happiness and peace in your life later. Know this: **You will get past this.**

You may not realize it at this moment, but you will have new people come into your life that will be very significant. You may have children or grandchildren in the future, a new love interest, a new best friend, a new opportunity, just around the corner. Hold on to the mystery and wonder of the future. It will come, God will see to that for you. It just may be difficult for you to see it from where you are on the journey. But you are moving forward.

"Let your eyes look directly forward, and your gaze be straight before you. Ponder the path of your feet; then all your ways will be sure. Do not swerve to the right or to the left; turn your foot away from evil" Proverbs 4: 25-27

Heavenly Father, thank you for supporting me while I move on my journey. Thank you for sending others into my life to keep me company. Amen.

Improperly Blaming Something or Someone

When we feel wronged or that something unwarranted has happened to us, we search for the reason. Who did this to us? We use blame to target our anger outward on to someone else.

"I have said these things to you, that in me you may have peace. In the world you will have tribulation. But take heart; I have overcome the world" John 16:33.

In the verse above, Jesus is quoted in the book of John as He spoke to his disciples. He wanted them to understand that, as Christians, they would have many tests and trials because they believed in Jesus when most people did not during that era. Regardless of the tribulations, Jesus told them not to worry because they would ultimately have peace in their lives. Like the disciples, you too will have a more peaceful future.

Early in your journey, you may feel the need to blame others or yourself. Blame is an enemy of progress on your journey. Blame is not helpful in any way. If trauma was inflicted on you or a loved one, if a loved one became ill or received an unsettling diagnosis, you may blame a host of other people or events. If you or an individual suffered an accident resulting in injury, blame might be an instant thought. Attorneys constantly advertise that they can help you earn money by blaming people. But blame is counterproductive. Blame will keep you stuck. To move beyond blame, you must think about judgment. You are being a judge when you assign blame. It may seem like you cannot stop judging and blaming yourself. This may be an ongoing struggle for you. If it takes you a while to move beyond blame, that is not unusual. But let's take a look at judgment, and we can revisit it again later in your journey.

"So then each of us will give an account of himself to God" Romans 14:12

As the verse written by the Apostle Paul states, we will all stand before God and give an account to God. Therefore, we are not to be concerned with judging or blaming others. The person you are blaming will stand before God and will be judged. Judgment is only to be done by God. Turn this over to Him as soon as you can. If you are not ready yet, that is ok. You may still feel someone else is to blame. You are not ready yet to let go of the blame. You are only being introduced to this idea now. Tuck the idea away for later in your journey, when you are ready. Self-blame may be even more difficult to let go of and forgiving yourself may be the most difficult task. We will visit this again later in the journey as well. So, do not feel bad if this takes some time. But know this: **all of the time and energy you spend on blame will slow you down on your journey back to God and peacefulness.** So, for now, concentrate on the following steps: read the words below, then close your eyes and think only about these words written by the James, the brother of Jesus:

> *"Draw near to God, and he will draw near to you..."*
> *James 4:8*

Read those words again. Take a slow deep breath and think about the words one more time.

Now read the words below:

> *"The Lord is near to all who call on him, to all who call on him in truth" Psalm 145:18*

Now you know. You have thought about God. You have drawn closer to Him, and He will be nearer to you because you called on Him. God is with you. You may not be ready yet to pray or have deeper feelings about God. Just remember He is patient, He will wait until you are ready. He will bring you peace in your life once again. His hand is still outstretched to you.

Heavenly Father, thank you for your patience. Thank you for not giving up on me as I walk through this difficult path. Please continue to guide and strengthen me. Amen.

Anxiety and Worry

"Therefore do not be anxious about tomorrow, for tomorrow will be anxious for itself. Sufficient for the day is its own trouble" Matthew 6:34

"Anxiety in a man's heart weights him down, but a good word makes him glad" Proverbs 12:25

There are many reasons you may be worried or have anxiety. These feelings often accompany trauma or significant events. Why? Remember that this event had an impact on your life. Somehow, your life was changed. You realized earlier on this journey that this event was out of your control. Anxiety and worry accompany a loss of control. A loss of "normalcy."

If you were a victim of a crime or accidental injury, anxiety would come along because you fear it may happen again. If these feelings of anxiety are significant, remember to contact a counselor or pastor. Anxiety may require additional support to assist you in reducing the symptoms of anxiety.

Worry and anxiety may be magnified after a trauma. It may help to think through the worry or anxiety that you are feeling and see if there are steps you can take to reduce the anxiety. If you lost a loved one or are now caring for a loved one, some of your worries may be financial. If so, seek help from friends and family who can help you reason through the financial steps you may need to take. Making a plan will help reduce the worry because you will begin to have some sense of control or management of this aspect of your life. The same is true for other areas of your life that are causing you to feel worried. If you are having to move as a result of the trauma or life-changing events, take time to plan the steps you need to take. If possible, make checklists or other concrete plans and ask others to assist as needed. Taking action to move forward will relieve the anxiety and worry you may be experiencing.

Jesus taught us about worry in the verse above from Matthew. He reminds us that worrying about details will not add any time to our lives and that there is more to life than worrying. Following the event that happened in your life, do not worry too far into the future but rather take your planning and worrying one day at a time. Take small steps then notice the progress you are making. Be thankful for any help you might receive from friends and family. God put those people in your path for a reason. Rely on them when you can and show your gratitude. This is also noted in the second verse above from Proverbs. Anxiety and worry will weigh on you but saying good words, thinking grateful thoughts, will lighten your heart and mind.

When you are feeling weak, worried, or anxious, Know this: **God is waiting there to help you.** If you are moving a little closer to God at this point in your journey, remember the verses below and think of these as you make progress in your daily plans and in your faith journey.

"I can do all things through Him who strengthens me" *Philippians 4:13.*

How can you get the strength you need?

"But Jesus looked at them and said, 'With man this is impossible, but with God all things are possible'" Matthew 19:26

Heavenly Father, thank you for my many blessings you have provided to me. Please give me strength and courage and help me with my worries. Amen.[4]

---

[4] HOPE AND HELP - How Can You Deal With Anxiety?
http://tiny.cc/te32sy

Feelings of Guilt

"Therefore, since we have been justified by faith, we have peace with God through our Lord Jesus Christ" Romans 5:1

"...casting all your anxieties on him, because he cares for you" 1 Peter 5:7

You are continuing on your journey by opening this book each day and reading these words. This is an indication that, even though you have undergone a trial, a significant test, you want to move forward and reconnect or move closer to God. You desire to feel at peace again. But you also may wrestle with guilt. You may feel that there was something you could have done to prevent the trauma or tragedy from happening. This is related to two other concepts: blame and anxiety. You might recall, in an earlier devotional, blame was related to judgment. Self-blame indicates that you are judging yourself about what happened in the past and have found yourself to be guilty. You judged that what happened was your fault or that you could have prevented it from occurring. Remember that only God is able to judge, so put that behind you and begin to move forward. As the Apostle Paul wrote in the verse above, we are justified by our faith, and therefore we have peace with God through Jesus. Do not burden yourself after the fact with guilt or self-blame. We all have been given the gift of peace although at times you may still feel uneasiness, self-blame, or guilt.

Guilt is also related to worry. How? Because if you still are blaming yourself at any level at all, then you are worrying that you should have done something differently. You worry that there was something you did or did not do in the scenario. You worry that "if only I had..." or "If only I hadn't" then things would have been better, or the event would not have happened at all. These thoughts will breed more worry and anxiety. As stated in the verse above, we are instructed to cast all anxieties on God because He cares for us. And because He cares, He will worry for us, and He will be the judge for us. We are accountable to him only. Do not worry about what you did or didn't do and do not attempt to judge or blame. Casting all of your worry about this on God will free you from a very heavy load.

Like blame, guilt will slow down your progress on your journey back to God. Guilt will spend your time and mental energy and will block your forward movement. Guilt will increase the likelihood that you will continue to have feelings of depression. Know this: **guilt is a heavy weight that God can help you lift off of your shoulders.** Let Him.

> *"Cast your burden on the Lord, and he will sustain you; he will never permit the righteous to be moved"* Psalm 55:22

> *"The Lord upholds all who are falling and raises up all who are bowed down"* Psalm 145:14

Heavenly Father, thank you for taking on all of my anxiety and worry. Please help me to remember that this is no longer my burden to bear. Amen.[5]

---

[5] Your Feelings Don't Have to Control You
http://tiny.cc/ro32sy

Intense Feelings of Shame

"But the Lord God helps me; therefore I have not been disgraced; therefore I have set my face like a flint, and I know that I shall not be put to shame" Isaiah 50:7

"I sought the Lord, and he answered me and delivered me from all my fears. Those who look to him are radiant, and their faces shall never be ashamed" Psalm 34: 4-5

Some types of traumas or tragedies may cause feelings of shame. Shame may come to a parent whose child, by making wrong choices, has altercations with the legal system. Shame may be the feeling a person has following abuse, whether physical, mental, or sexual abuse or assault. Shame may be the result of past legal problems that you may have experienced. It may also be the feeling you have when if a person believed an accident or tragedy could have been prevented, yet since the tragedy happened, and you feel ashamed about not preventing it. Shame may be a feeling also associated with self-guilt and blame.

The verses above clearly tell the reader that God helps you to work through feelings of shame and that believers shall not experience shame. Yet shame can be an underlying lingering feeling that you may have difficulty shaking. Shame is another feeling associated with anxiety. This is because you may have underlying shame about the past and worry what other people are hearing about the events. If the past tragedy is already known by others, you may worry about what they think of you and the tragedy. You may think they are blaming you. In other words, you are worrying about their judgment of you. The second verse underscores the importance of looking to God because those who do, regardless of the past, shall never be ashamed.

Shame is also a feeling that can sneak up on you even though you are working to move closer to God. The feeling of shame that you have may cause you to think that you cannot be close to God. But as the verse from Isaiah states, being close to God will mean that you will not experience shame. Things that others may say, or perhaps your perception or interpretation of what others are saying, will trigger the feeling of shame. Know this: **God will lift you up and provide meaningful positive experiences that you will be able to focus on as you continue on your journey.** Look forward. Be thankful for the time you are using to read devotionals and learn more about God's love and support for those who need Him.

"For the Scripture says, 'Everyone who believes in him will not be put to shame'" Romans 10:11

"But you, O Lord, are a shield about me, my glory, and the lifter of my head" Psalm 3:3

Heavenly Father, thank you for being with me. Thank you for helping me with my feelings of shame and guilt. Please keep me near you when I worry. Amen.[6]

---

[6] BEING GUIDED THROUGH LIFE AS YOU STUDY THROUGH GOD'S WORD
http://tiny.cc/8t32sy

Relationship of Anxiety, Worry, Guilt, and Shame

"For God gave us a spirit not of fear but of power and love and self-control" 2 Timothy 1:7.

Following trauma or tragedy, you may have a tangled web of emotions that you have difficulty sorting out. Of the major feelings often experienced, anxiety, sadness, or depression are commonly found. Depending on the particular type of trauma or tragedy you experienced, you may also have feelings of guilt and shame. Worry will likely be among the feelings you have. If you have the feelings of anxiety, worry, guilt, and shame, it is important to note that these feelings are interrelated and often feed off of one another. You may benefit from examining Appendix 3 which shows you how these feelings are related.

Anxiety about a trauma or event can easily transfer to everyday worry. Perhaps you never used to be a "worrier" before this event. But now you find yourself worrying. You may also worry what others think about the event, your ability to handle the trauma, or that people even believe you could have done something differently (guilt). Guilt can certainly lead to shame about the past events. These types of emotions reinforce each other. What does this mean? It means that the more often you are engaging in one of these thought patterns, the more likely this endless cycle of negative emotions will continue. This cycle of anxiety, worry, guilt, and shame, can lead you to depression and sadness.

The verse above was written in a letter by the Apostle Paul to a young believer that he mentored. He told Timothy to be brave in his actions and not to fear because God gave us a spirit of power, love, and self-control. We are to focus our minds on God's power, love, and exercise self-control. This self-control can include our own thoughts. When you feel that you are going into the endless cycle of negative thoughts, you can ask God for strength and help to move forward.

"Peace I leave with you; my peace I give you. Not as the world gives do I give to you. Let not your hearts be troubled, neither let them be afraid" John 14:27.

As this passage clearly tells us, Jesus has given us peace even greater than the worries of our own world. Calling on God will assist you in letting go of your troubled heart and turning fear away. Know this: **when you ask God to give you strength and help you to see blessings, you will not be thinking negative thoughts.** He can help you break the cycle.

"I sought the Lord and he answered me and delivered me from all my fears" Psalm 34:4

Heavenly Father, please continue to give me strength to travel on this journey with you. Help me to see all of the blessings you have given to me. Amen.

Awareness of God and Residual Anger

"They are darkened in their understanding, alienated from the life of God because of the ignorance that is in them, due to their hardness of heart" Ephesians 4:18

This verse was written to explain to believers that there are some people, typically those who are not Christians, who simply do not understand the glory of God and His son, Jesus. He further points out that these individuals have a hardness of heart.

"And how from childhood you have been acquainted with the sacred writings, which are able to make you wise for salvation through faith in Christ Jesus" 2 Timothy 3:15

In this verse written to Timothy, Paul reminds him that he was well aware of the sacred writings of Scriptures from childhood and this will help in understanding the grace given to us all through Christ. Both of these verses can be applied to the difficulties people experience when they do not fully understand the total grace of God and how He accepts all those who ask for acceptance and forgiveness. As you travel down this pathway toward God, it will be helpful to think about the love that God has for you no matter what.

There is no road map for the journey you are on. It has probably been riddled with sadness, anger, anxiety, shock, disbelief, and many other emotions. It has probably been a bumpy ride. You may not have had many good days yet. But you are still moving forward. Rejoice that you are working hard to make progress and rejoice that you are continuing to seek God.

During this journey, you may have conflicting feelings about God or your faith. You may still have some feelings of anger toward God because this event happened in your life. But you may also have less anger toward God than you did when you began on this journey. You may have rekindled some feelings of faith or knowledge of God from earlier years and previous experiences that were positive. As Paul reminded Timothy, you have a foundation with God. Your initial foundation with God is still there.

How can you have multiple feelings about God and your faith all at the same time you are harboring feelings of anger with God? God is a gracious and loving God. He allows you to work through this part of your faith journey knowing that you are still loved by Him. Know this: **You are a child of the King, and He will not forget you, especially in your time of sorrow or trouble.** You might ask: How can this be? He believes in you and is not finished working with you. He wants you to return to an even stronger faith than before the trauma.

> *"He saved us, not because of works done by us in righteousness, but according to his own mercy, by the washing of regeneration and renewal of the Holy Spirit"* Titus 3:5

To help you move forward, think about the gifts given to you for which you have not even thought to ask: a sunrise, spring rains, winter snows, flowering plants, lively animals, people who love you and support you. God is good; you are blessed. You will keep riding along on this journey and will reach the destination of peacefulness in your life and with God.

Heavenly Father, I confess I may have had a hardened heart after all of these happenings in my life. I pray for your love to keep me strong and help me through this time. Amen.

Searching for Happiness

"For everyone who asks receives, and the one who seeks finds, and to the one who knocks it will be opened"
Matthew 7:8

"But seek first the kingdom of God and his righteousness, and all these things will be added to you"
Matthew 6:33

In an earlier devotional, you read about our human need to "fix" things, to make things better after a tragedy or traumatic event. In this effort, we may move, change jobs, go on a trip to get away from the place of the tragedy, or other life-changing strategies. These efforts may buy us time and space, but these efforts are not going to help us reach our destination of peacefulness. We are mistaken to think these activities will take the place of peace with ourselves and with God.

You will eventually discover that the real answer you are searching for is peacefulness with God. What you are searching for is to be closer once again to the Lord and to walk with Him each day as you move forward. He alone is the true helper to move you along on your journey. Why? Because He can alleviate your worry, guilt, anxiety, and shame. Walking in the way that Jesus has instructed, to be more like Him will re-establish peacefulness in your heart. Walking with Him means looking at the wonderful gifts in your life rather than thinking about tragedy day in and day out. Walking with Him means thinking about how you might be of service to others and how the tragedy you experienced may make you a better servant to others and God.

You might now be asking, "How do I get there? How can I be sure that I am walking and living my life as He instructed?" There are some fairly simple steps that you can take each day that will assist you in moving forward. Read devotionals and the Bible. When you feel you are taking a wrong turn down the road of despair or anxiety, turn to the passages that comfort you. Think intently about how you can apply each passage to your own personal life. As you are reading these passages, take notes, write down what living in this way would look like for you. Would it mean that, rather than thinking negative or anxious thoughts about the past, you would think about the example set before us by Jesus? Would it mean that you would begin to love yourself again? Would it mean that you would begin to think about not blaming others, yourself, and perhaps thinking about forgiveness? We will visit all of these strategies in the coming devotionals. But for now, know this: **when reading the word of God, you are not thinking negative thoughts, you are thinking of Him.** Let God help you with this process. He is walking beside you each day. He is waiting and watching for the exact moment when you feel Him wash over you with kindness and warmth. It will happen.

"I love those who love me, and those who seek me diligently find me" Proverbs 8:17

Heavenly Father, help me to stay close to you by reading the Scriptures. Guide me on the path that I am on and help me to remain strong. Amen.

Moving on from Shame and Guilt

"The thief comes only to steal and kill and destroy. I came that they may have life and have it abundantly" John 10:10

"Look at the birds of the air: they neither sow nor reap nor gather into barns, and yet your heavenly Father feeds them. Are you not of more value than they? Matthew 6:26

You continue to read your Scriptures and devotionals as you travel on this journey. There comes the point on the road where you will need to stop and take a good long hard look backward and see what you have left behind. By now, you have begun to move closer to God and, as time goes by, you are moving further in time from the event or trauma. You have made much progress. You are understanding more about how to live beyond the tragedy and how to move forward. At this point in time, you will need to consider moving away from all shame and guilt. Why is this so important? It is important because hanging on to these emotions and thoughts prevents us from receiving true forgiveness and peacefulness. Hanging on to these thoughts encourages negative, dark thoughts. These types of thoughts can increase other negative thoughts and emotions, such as anger.

In the first verse, Jesus said that those who did not believe in Christ would be tempted to go in the wrong direction, but those who believe would be saved. Think about applying this to your current situation. When you are not acting as God intends, you may entertain negative thoughts, emotions, and behaviors, and increase the likelihood of other sins, such as blaming others or not forgiving others. Jesus came so that we would have abundant lives. Even though we have suffered tests, trauma, or tragedy, it is not God's wish for us to live in despair thinking negative thoughts about ourselves or others. You are of great value to God. As stated in the second verse, God cares for all living creatures, but He cares most for us.

How do we move away from guilt and shame? Remember that shame is an emotion that only you can see in yourself, that only you can feel about yourself and the past events. Others do not see shame; others do not sense your feelings of guilt that you have placed upon you. There may have been nothing at all that you could have done differently in past events that would have made a better outcome. Most events or tragedies in life are a culmination of several factors, which you do not control. So, let those feelings go. Perhaps you are saying "But I know I could have done_____" differently. If, for whatever reason, you feel a strong need to confess to God that you could have done something differently, then confess it right away, and you will be forgiven. That is it. Seems simple enough? It is. Know this: **God forgives you when you confess.** Not only will you be forgiven, but you will also be cleansed. Confess it, receive it. Move forward.

"If we confess our sins, he is faithful and just to forgive us our sins and to cleanse us from all unrighteousness" 1 *John 1:9*

Heavenly Father, I know that you are in control of all things. Please forgive me for any wrongdoing I may have committed and take this burden of shame or guilt from my heart. Amen.

We Must Resist Isolation

"Whoever isolates himself seeks his own desire; he breaks out against all sound judgment" Proverbs 18:1

"By this we know that we abide in him and he in us, because he has given us of his Spirit" 1 John 4:13

Tragedy and trauma leave you wanting to avoid going places and being with people. You may have initially accepted help from family and friends, perhaps you even requested it. But as time moves on, you may find yourself wanting to be alone. You may believe that others will want to dwell on the trauma or ask you questions about things you do not want to talk about. Or, you may think you have nothing in common with others who have not had to endure these significant tests, even though you used to be good friends or spend a great deal of time together before the trauma.

During the first part of the journey, you may have needed time and space alone. It was a shock, it was not planned, and your world became a different place because of the tragedy. You have experienced that pause, the break from others, to collect yourself and begin to sort out your new life. Part of the new life will be associating with people. You may want to reconnect with those you knew before and during the traumatic event. Or, you may want to find others to visit with and establish new relationships. You do not need to find a large group of people and jump right in the middle of the group, but you should be seeking the company of one or two or three close friends by now. These social events need not be all day long affairs but get out there and have a cup of coffee, a meal, a conversation. Go to church with friends or go to a church function. Contact other Christians who can support you. As the first verse states, to seek isolation is not good judgment.

Do not worry about socializing. It will not be as difficult as you might think. Remember that God intended for us to have companions and to be brothers and sisters in Christ. He encourages this fellowship. It is perfectly fine to take it slowly. Perhaps only one or two outings a week at first. Do not have anxiety about these initial outings. As with other things you do in your life, God is with you so set your worries aside.

> "It is the Lord who goes before you. He will be with you; he will not leave you or forsake you. Do not fear or be dismayed" Deuteronomy 31:8

Before Moses died, he gave instructions to Joshua about taking the people to the promised land. The verse above is what Moses told Joshua, so as to alleviate his fears. When you are going into a new or different situation, think about Joshua. He knew that going forward; God was with him as He is with you.

Other than being around people for socialization and decreasing feelings of loneliness, there is another more important reason not to isolate yourself. Know this: **being with other friends of faith will encourage your own spiritual growth.** Remember that your final destination is peacefulness with God. Having friends who are strong in their faith will assist you on your journey. Being around people with true faith in God will strengthen your positive outlook and the time spent with these friends will be time you will not be worrying or feeling sadness or anxiety. Once you have made these connections, take the opportunity to visit often. You and the company you keep will both be blessed.

Heavenly Father, guide me to find the support and friendships that will help me. Thank you for staying close to me as I move forward. Amen. [7]

---

[7] How Does Knowledge of God's Personality Help Us to Change? http://tiny.cc/im42sy

Seeking Others So You Can Receive the Needed Help and Encouragement

"Two are better than one, because they have a good reward for their toil. For if they fall, one will lift up his fellow. But woe to him who is alone when he falls and has not another to lift him up!" Ecclesiastes 4:9

"That is, that we may be mutually encouraged by each other's faith, both yours and mine" Romans 1:12

Walking through your faith journey, you have experienced many emotions. Initially, you may have wanted more time alone. As discussed in the devotional about isolation, being with others may benefit you and the other person. But you may have questions about how to find people that will support you or, if you already have a good basis of support with family and friend, you may wish to know how to establish even stronger relationships with others. This may seem more complicated than before the tragedy. You are beginning to feel a need to be with others, yet things are different now, and you may not wish to seem a burden to friends. One thing to think about is planning activities or gatherings in which you are all participating equally. These gatherings may center around meals together, church gatherings, movies, walks, runs, picnics, and so on. In each of these, everyone has the opportunity to participate equally. When you participate in such events, you may feel that you are beginning to socialize in the same way you socialized before the trauma. This is a giant step forward on your journey. Why is socializing so important? The Bible instructs us to do so.

The first verse of this devotional points out once again that we are to maintain friendships so that we can mutually help each other. It also indicates that either person in a friendship may need help and that, even though you have experienced a trauma or tragedy, you should provide help to others as they need it. These acts of kindness and support will move you steadily forward in our faith journey.

The second verse of Scripture underscores the importance of friendships in strengthening faith. Your association with others will strengthen their faith just as they will strengthen your faith. In other words, we all should look out for each other and reinforce each other's faith. If you feel you are not far enough on your faith journey to be offering strength to others, then others may strengthen you more and eventually, you will strengthen others' faith.

Your past experiences will give you strength, knowledge, and empathy for life experiences that you have never had before. As your faith strengthens, you will need this empathy to continue living as expected by God.

"Bear one another's burdens, and so fulfill the law of Christ" Galatians 6:2

Heavenly Father, thank you for providing me with opportunities to be with others. Help me to support others when they are in need. Amen.

Allowing Others in Your Life

"This is my commandment, that you love one another as I have loved you" John 15:12

"Give, and it will be given to you. Good measure, pressed down, shaken together, running over, will be put into your lap. For with the measure you use it will be measured back to you" Luke 6:38

Your journey continues. Jesus issued a commandment in the book of John stating that we should love one another. It is His wish for us to all be united and help each other according to the way He helped others. His life set an example for us to follow. This may be difficult to think about and to do if you are still wrestling with your own relationship with God or with other people. In truth, God sends people to us that we need. It is amazing the people God will put in your path that can help you along. These individuals will be people that you can easily relate to, and they will be reaching out to you. How will you know? Watch for a kind word or deed, a comment that lets you know they are sensing your feelings, or statements that signal you have things in common that will move you toward a closer relationship with each other and with God. These individuals may have been in your life before your tragedy, but you did not need them in the same way. Recall this journey actually began before the event? The initial devotional asked that you think about how your life was before the tragedy happened and to realize that there were people you might need to call on for support. In the past, some of these individuals may have only been acquaintances. They may be neighbors or people you met in the community or at work. Be watchful that they might be attempting to support you now and establish a helping relationship.

The second verse above reminds us that the way we give or interact, will be given back to us. In fact, it says it will be put in your lap! This is another way of saying it will be placed before you. This verse can mean if we are not being positive with others, they will not be positive with us. Or, when we act positively, the same will happen to us. When you see these opportunities for connecting, take them and interact with others.

You have known of the ten commandments in the old testament. But when Jesus was asked about commandments, He gave us two. The first was to love God. The second was to love your neighbor as yourself. In times when you feel stressed or disconnected, know this: **others are ready to offer this type of love to you and, as Jesus said, you are to love them as well.**

> *"'The second is this: You shall love your neighbor as yourself.' There is no other commandment greater than these" Mark 12:31*

Heavenly Father, thank you for putting people in my path. Help me to know how to ask for support and how to offer it back to others. Amen.

Anniversaries and Other Celebrations

"Blessed are those who mourn, for they shall be comforted" Matthew 5:4

"For everything there is a season, and a time for every matter under heaven: a time to be born, and a time to die; a time to plant, and to pluck up what is planted; a time to kill, and a time to heal; a time to break down, and a time to build up; a time to weep, and a time to laugh; a time to mourn, and a time to dance..." Ecclesiastes 3:1-4

One year from the time of the tragedy, and possibly every year after that, you and others around you will think about the anniversary of the event. It may feel like you have stepped backward on your journey quite a bit. You may mentally relive the event or when you heard the news of the event. You may feel many of the same emotions that you felt on that day and for the days after the event: depression, anxiety, sadness, worry, a sense that things will never be the same. Do not be surprised by these feelings. You may want to revisit some of the earlier devotionals that address these feelings. Perhaps you will go a step or two backward on the journey, but this is an excellent opportunity to allow those around you to support you. It is a time to also think about the many blessings you have even after the event.

Reaching an anniversary is a chance to look back to see the progress you have made since then. You have moved forward through the initial pain and shock. You have gradually been moving forward toward others and toward God. These are all milestones that you can recognize and appreciate.

In addition to the anniversary of the actual event, you may also take a step backward during important celebrations that you enjoyed prior to the tragedy. Perhaps Christmas, birthdays, or other personal celebrations, may be particularly rough during the first year or more. If the tragedy was the loss of a loved one, you will think back to the holidays and memories you had with that person before they passed away. If the tragedy was a divorce, miscarriage, or other personal relationship tragedy or trauma, you will think about those occurrences during the celebrations and holidays.

The second verse above is such an important one to think about during these difficult days. There will be times that you will mourn, cry, breakdown, and there will equally be times to celebrate birth, to laugh, dance, and to be healed. You are moving through both good and bad times, and your emotions will be influenced. Remember that your mind and your thoughts can begin a negative cycle if you continue to think about the negative thoughts for days after these celebrations. It is ok to reflect on the anniversary or holiday, and then, as in the past, refer to positive Bible passages, uplifting friends, social activities, and review the blessings of your life. Know this: **each anniversary or holiday will gradually become easier to bear if you take God's hand to walk through these times.** He will heal you. Ask Him for the help you need.

"He heals the broken hearted and binds up their wounds" Psalm 147:3

Heavenly Father, help me to be strong. I pray for your strength and love. Help me to remember that with you I will have a peaceful life in my future. Amen.

Is it OK to be Happy?

"Even in laughter the heart may ache, and the end of joy may be grief" Proverbs 14:13

"A joyful heart is good medicine, but a crushed spirit dries up the bones" Proverbs 17:22

"Also that everyone should eat and drink and take pleasure in all his toll-this is God's gift to man" Ecclesiastes 3:13

It might be an unusual thought that crosses your mind along this journey. You may actually wonder if it is OK for you to feel happy. Perhaps you think enough time has not passed. You may think you are supposed to remain sad or to struggle with moving on in your journey past the tragedy. Why would you have these feelings? Some people state that they feel guilty about being happy. Since this tragedy happened, they should somehow be punished by not experiencing happiness for a long, long, time, if ever.

The first verse reminds us that you may have laughter and happiness at the same time. Your heart is not completely healed yet you can smile or laugh at times. It is perfectly fine to have the emotions of happiness and excitement. You should laugh and seek contentment and enjoyment in life. In fact, as you see in the second verse of Proverbs, laughter can actually be helpful in moving your spirit to a better place.

Along the line of experiencing happiness, perhaps it is time on this journey for you to begin to plan activities that you will enjoy. Begin to look for happy events and occasions. Look for activities that you have enjoyed in the past and experience those again. As the verse from Ecclesiastes tells us, we are to celebrate and enjoying events because God has given this to us as a gift. Know this: **God expects us to enjoy our lives rather than to continue living in grief with a crushed spirit.** You have been traveling further and further in your faith journey. Looking for enjoyment and, experiencing laughter again, are on the route you are traveling. Stop along this route and participate and then count these experiences among your blessings.

> *"Then our mouth was filled with laughter, and our tongue with shouts of joy; then they said among the nations, 'The Lord has done great things for them'" Psalm 126:2*

Heavenly Father, Thank you for my many blessings. Help me to see the joy in life and to restore the cheer in my heart. Amen.

Coping with the Pain of Unexpected Reminders

"Keep me as the apple of your eye; hide me in the shadow of your wings" Psalm 17:8

"But the Lord is faithful. He will establish you and guard you against the evil one" 2 Thessalonians 3:3

"Though I walk in the midst of trouble, you preserve my life; you stretch out your hand against the wrath of my enemies, and your right hand delivers me" Psalm 138:7

As discussed in an earlier devotional, there are days or occasions that might be difficult to handle, such as anniversaries or holidays. When you reach these days or celebrations along your journey, refer to Bible passages to find strength and to help you move on to the next day. But there may be unexpected reminders in your environment, such as news media, locations where you remember something about the tragedy, even people you associated with the tragedy. Someone may say something unprovoked, that may cause the memories to rush back into your mind. You may not know what to say or how to respond to such comments. You may feel stunned, angry, panicked, frustrated, depressed, all over again. You may be completely speechless.

It might be best to think ahead to some situations like this so that you will be prepared with a strategy. How do you react? What would you say back? How would you handle other types of reminders such as a news report, visiting a location again, or any unexpected visual reminders? It is important to think about ahead of time so that you do not react in such a way that your emotions may begin to tumble out of control and your resort back to the negative thought cycle again.

One strategy is to find a favorite verse, prayer, saying, or song, to think about. As stated in the verses above, God will protect you. Visualize the image of the first verse, of being protected beneath God's wing. It would be comforting to feel that overarching protection of God surrounding you. The second verse states that

God will indeed protect you from "the evil one." The evil one includes the dark spirit that fights for your attention against God's positive love. You have been fighting against this negativity since you began the journey. All the while, God can protect you from this when you ask.

And the third verse reminds you that, even though you might be walking right into danger, by being in a location associated with the tragedy or by interacting with someone who seeks to harm your spirit by saying things about the event, God will protect you. He will help you through these unexpected reminders of your trauma. Once the reminder has passed, take a deep breath, say the verse or prayer that you have already put into your arsenal or toolkit, and move beyond the reminder. You are not in a safe vacuum where there will never be a reminder. These reminders will likely turn up now and again. Strategize so you will not be caught off guard. Have a plan in place. And, then check your thoughts to be sure you are not falling back into a negative thought pattern. Know this: **God will protect you from these dark thoughts when you ask Him to do so.**

"The name of the Lord is a strong tower; the righteous man runs into it and is safe" Proverbs 18:10

Heavenly Father, Thank you for your love each day. Please keep me strong when I am tempted to fall back into weakness. Keep me from despair. Amen.

Stress in Relationships

"My inward parts are in turmoil and never still; days of affliction come to meet me" Job 30:27

"Be angry and do not sin; do not let the sun go down on your anger" Ephesians 4:26

Having a significant tragedy happen in your life has put you through a difficult test. You have had so many emotions flooding in over the past steps of your journey since the event. When we are on emotional roller coasters, our whole demeanor changes or fluctuates in ways that we cannot predict or even understand. As we interact with others, our feelings may show. We may give responses or react in ways that we would never have thought of prior to the tragedy. When others reach out, we may withdraw. When others attempt to lighten our thoughts, we may become angry thinking "They cannot possibly understand." We may resent that others are experiencing joy and happiness. We may become easily irritated with others. We may remain angry with people who mean well. As the second verse reminds us, we should not hold grudges, and we should continue to harbor anger.

These feelings can specifically impact the relationships we have had with others prior to the event. If the event caused conflict between a husband and wife, usually due to casting blame, then marital discord, separation, or even thoughts of divorce may follow. These are things that you would never have entertained prior to the event. But now, you may think about these divisive actions as real possibilities. If the tragedy caused conflict between you and your parents, siblings, or even very close friends, these wounds might continue to impact your relationships shortly after the event.

These painful interactions with and reactions to each other cause more stress than you think you can bear. Sometimes the best thing to do during these times is to be still, pray, and wait.

"The Lord will fight for you, and you have only to be silent" Exodus 14:14

This sounds easier than it may feel to you at the time. Remember that God made our spirits capable of controlling our thoughts and words. It may take a great deal of effort and time to move beyond this level of stress within a relationship. You probably have heard of family members who have not spoken to each other for many years. Don't allow this to happen in your own relationships. Healing relationships is an area of your life that may require more time to mend. Be patient. God is patient with you and sets a good example for us. As you are working on this, consult your Bible for Scripture that has meaning for you. Say prayers, prayers that request the strength and knowledge of how to work with this situation. Pray that you, and the other person in the relationship, will be given the knowledge from God of how to resolve the stress. Know this: **God wants you to request help and He will lift you up.**

"When the cares of my heart are many, your consolations cheer my soul" Psalm 94:19

"I have set the Lord always before me; because he is at my right hand, I shall not be shaken" Psalm 16:8

Heavenly Father, please bring peace to our hearts so that we may put our conflicts behind us. Guide us in our actions toward each other. Amen.[8]

---

[8] Cultivate a Lasting Love That Never Fails
http://tiny.cc/6242sy
Why Pausing Before You Speak Does Not Really Work
http://tiny.cc/x442sy

Questions from Others

"Do not be overcome by evil, but overcome evil with good" Romans 12:21

"A soft answer turns away wrath, but a harsh word stirs up anger" Proverbs 15:1

"But I say to you, love your enemies and pray for those who persecute you" Matthew 5:44

You read about unexpected reminders of the trauma in an earlier devotional. Those reminders might catch you by surprise. But sometimes, even more alarming, are the blunt questions that people may ask. When you are feeling especially sensitive about the past events, such as shortly after the event or during a holiday or anniversary when your feelings are raw, these questions may be hurtful. You may perceive the questions as intentionally ugly. And some may be. Perhaps the other person has evil motivation for asking direct questions. It will be helpful to prepare for such interactions ahead of time if possible. If you have already had these experiences, you may need to analyze how you reacted to the questions to determine if your reaction was an acceptable reaction.

The verses above address ways to react. These verses remind us that, even though an individual attacked us in some way, we should not respond in kind. We should make an effort to overcome any evil intentions with positive reactions. We are told in the second verse that if we react in a similar unpleasant way, our harsh words can stir up even more anger. We are also asked to pray for individuals who have evil intentions toward us. This is hard. We are asked to pray for the other person because we should want to help them move the evilness out of their heart. But praying for the other person is helpful to us as well because now we have switched our evil defensive thoughts to positive, loving thoughts for another person. When we encounter such questions, a wonderful strategy would be to commit these words to memory and to call upon this verse:

"Let the words of my mouth and the mediation of my heart be acceptable in your sight, O Lord, my rock and my redeemer" Psalm 19:14

Although it may feel like questions asked about the trauma are uncomfortable, and that the person may be asking with evil intention, some people ask questions such as these out of concern for you. They may be worried about your welfare and how you are moving along after such a traumatic event. This is another reason we must employ a positive rather than a defensive or angry reaction. Know this: **God will give you guidance and strength through His words to react as you should.**

"Love one another with brotherly affection. Outdo one another in showing honor" Romans 12:10

Heavenly Father, please help me to understand that people do not always have bad intentions. And Lord, if a person has a bad intention, please take the evilness from their heart and from mine. Amen.

Why?

"Count it all joy, my brothers, when you meet trials of various kinds, for you know that the testing of your faith produces steadfastness. And let steadfastness have its full effect, that you may be perfect and complete, lacking nothing" James 1:2-4

"And we know that for those who love God all things work together for good, for those who are called according to his purpose" Romans 8:28

The question of why is one that every person who has experienced any form of tragedy or sadness about an event will ask. Why did it have to happen? Why to me? Why to my family member? Immediately following the tragedy, you were probably not able to read the passages above. These passages may have made you angry because you were likely experiencing anger about the event. You were likely angry at everyone and everything. You may have also been extremely angry with God. You may have experienced deep sadness. Now, as you have been traveling through your journey past the trauma, you might be able to read the verses above without anger or sadness. This is tremendous progress on your journey!

Jesus's brother, James, wrote the first passage to new believers who were often tormented for their faith. He reminded them that the people who were acting against them were testing their faith and that they should remain strong in their Christian beliefs. The Apostle Paul wrote the second verse to remind believers that everything that was happening to them in the early church was for a bigger plan.

Depending on the type of trauma you experienced, there may be no reason at all that the tragedy happened. A loved one being diagnosed with a fatal disease and then experiencing their heavenly journey home. This was God's plan for that person, and finally, they are in a place without the disease. But other traumas, such as those in which another person was responsible for the tragedy, are more complicated to sort out. A crime was committed by another person to you or a loved one. A spouse is unfaithful, and divorce or separation results from this. Someone is abused by another person. These are all examples in which you are tested because of the evil intentions of another. These acts are particularly hard to process due to the anger and blame that may still exist. These types of events will be discussed in more detail in the devotionals addressing forgiveness.

In truth, humans cannot understand why particular events happen. These events can be the result of evil hearts, a culmination of several factors that result in tragic car accident or injury, or just the culmination of factors and the human condition of sinfulness. Regardless, we are to think about how we can count these tragedies among the events in our lives from which we will learn, and we will grow closer to God. We must remember that we are on God's clock. He will show us the meaningful plans for our future when we are ready to act upon those plans. We may continue to question why for many years and, ultimately, when we are living in peacefulness again, we will have a better understanding. Know this: **You will rejoice in the future when you are walking in the path God has planned for you!** Today, pray and be hopeful as noted in the verses below.

> *"Blessed is the man who remains steadfast under trial, for when he has stood the test he will receive the crown of life, which God has promised to those who love him"* James 1:12

> *"Rejoice in hope, be patient in tribulation, be constant in prayer"* Romans 12:12

Heavenly Father, help me to be strong during these difficult trials and tests. Thank you for the love you have given to me. Amen.

Awareness of God's Presence in my Life

"Now faith is the assurance of things hoped for, the conviction of things not seen. For by it the people of old received their commendation. By faith we understand that the universe was created by the word of God, so that what is seen was not made out of things that are visible" Hebrews 11: 1-3

"Jesus said to him, 'Have you believed because you have seen me? Blessed are those who have not seen and yet have believed'" John 20:29

For those who have undergone tragic experiences that many other people cannot even imagine, the presence of God in your life may be difficult to assume. You may have realized that you can pray to God, that He exists for others and you too can pray to him. But how do you know if He is present? And an even greater question is, how can you know He is really in your life right now? After all that you have been through and felt, how do you know that He is there now?

The verses above speak to us about faith in God who cannot be seen. We must remember that God has three important bodies within the one. God the Father, God the Holy Spirit, and His Son, Jesus. When we read passages, hear hymns or other music that is for praise and worship, listen to a sermon, and talk with other Christians, we sense there is a presence of God, who is greater than all of these experiences. Some people describe the sensing of the Holy Spirit within them when they participate in these activities. They may speak of feeling the warmth and freedom in their relationship with God since they know they are redeemed. But how do you know He is there for you?

We only need make observations of the world around to know there is a God and He is here with you. As you watch a baby grow, hear a child's first words, see a toddler walk, you know these are miracles and that God is within these tiny innocent humans. But we only need to watch the news to know that evil is also present in the world. Evil, in fact, lurks in every corner waiting to pounce on those who do not know God.

Let's think about this: You survived a terrible trauma. You began searching for answers to the questions about the tragedy. Why did it happen? What to do now? Why would God allow this? Is God really with you? You cannot see Him. You must proceed by faith alone. You could easily have turned to the evil ways of resolving your trauma. You could have reacted in a hostile manner. You could have remained in a deep depression. You could avoid all contact with all people. You could refuse to read Scripture. But you did not. You are here. Know this: **God is leading you down this path, and this is evidence that He is present in your life right now.** Hold on to Him. Ask him for strength. Be patient. Be kind to others. God is working within you.

"For by grace you have been saved through faith. And this is not your own doing; it is the gift of God" *Ephesians 2:8*

Heavenly Father, thank you for being present in my life. Help me to feel your presence and remain close to you. Amen.

It is Never Going to be "OK"

"So we can confidently say, 'The Lord is my helper; I will not fear; what can man do to me?" Hebrews 13:6

"And give no opportunity to the devil" Ephesians 4:27

"It does not rejoice at wrongdoing, but rejoices with the truth" 1 Corinthians 13: 6

Your past experience will never go away. It will never be OK that the tragedy happened. It may be hurtful to hear others say to you "But that was so long ago. Aren't you over that?" And the answer is no. You will never be "over that." It does not go away. Do not feel like you are failing because you are unable to get to the point where the past is forgotten. How could it be forgotten? It was the trial of your whole lifetime.

You will be able to move past the trauma as you continue down the faith journey. You can look back and still see it. It will never disappear. But you can continue to grow your faith and look forward more days than you look back. You will reach your peaceful life and still know that the tragedy is back there, miles away, but still there.

In order to be able to continue making this progress, the Scripture reminds us that God is our helper. He is walking beside you. You might forget He is there, but He will not forget you. When you are struggling, in your mind visualize that He is walking side-by-side with you. When you are feeling weak, He will hold you up. He will be there always. When you sense that you are having a weak moment, do not give any "opportunity to the devil" as noted in the second verse above. Allowing anger, blame, resentfulness, bitterness, sadness back into your thoughts is allowing the evilness to creep back in. These will be the times for you to pray for help.

On your journey, you should be moving toward the truth. When Paul wrote the verse above to the people in Corinth, he wanted them to understand the unconditional love that God has for us and that we should have for each other. He included this verse to say that love rejoices in the truth and does not seek to continue with doing the wrong thing. As Christians, we leave these wrongs in the past and strive always to do the right thing. Leave the wrongdoing behind you, far off in the distance, and move toward the truth that God loves you and is there to help. Know this: **When you ask God to help you, He will not leave you.** It will never be OK, but God will always be with you on your journey.

In the verse below, Joshua told the people that he would be with them just as he was with Moses. He wanted the people to know that he would be there for them. For you, God will be with you always to strengthen you.

> *"No man shall be able to stand before you all the days of your life. Just as I was with Moses, so I will be with you. I will not leave you or forsake you" Joshua 1:5*

Heavenly Father, thank you for your presence and love. Please hold my hand and keep me moving forward. Guide me in the way I need to go. Amen.

Leave God to the Judgment

"For the wrongdoer will be paid back for the wrong he has done, and there is no partiality" Colossians 3:25

"For we must all appear before the judgment seat of Christ, so that each one may receive what is due for what he has done in the body, whether good or evil" 2 Corinthians 5:10

Some types of tragedies involve actions committed by others toward you or a member of your family. At the beginning of this faith journey, you may have had strong feelings about the blame of others, the guilt of others, and the punishment of others. If the event you or your family experienced was a tragedy that involved the actions of another person or persons, it is easy to understand your feelings of blame and punishment. These feelings are plagued with anger and resentment toward others. These are strong feelings that are difficult to fight.

Judgment is something that likely has weighed heavily on your mind for some time.

But what if you knew for certain that the individual you are angry with, the one you believe is guilty, is guaranteed to be judged? As the Scripture tells us, that person will absolutely receive a proper judgment before God. There is no question about this. That individual will be judged and paid back according to the verses above. If there was an unjust act, God already knows this. Understanding that judgment is a certainty sheds a different light on previous thinking. In the past, you may have felt that judging this person was something you needed to be responsible for doing. You may have believed that it was your obligation to assure judgment somehow. Now you know that judgment is not yours to worry about; the person will be judged. Not only did you feel responsible for judgment, but you may have also believed it was up to you to arrange punishment of the person.

"Beloved, never avenge yourselves, but leave it to the wrath of God, for it is written, 'Vengeance is mine, I will repay, says the Lord'" Romans 12:19

"Do not say 'I will repay evil'; wait for the Lord, and he will deliver you" Proverbs 20:22.

These verses tell us directly that we are not supposed to worry about punishment or to pay another person back for their sins committed toward us or a loved one. Judgment and punishment are God's responsibility. The wonderful thing about realizing this is that now your mind can be free of this burden. Know this: **God will judge, and He will punish as needed**. If this weighed heavily upon you in the past, you should feel relief knowing all of these things will be taken care of in the future in a much more powerful and meaningful way than you would be able to do.

Heavenly Father, forgive me for wanting to judge and punish others. Please take this burden from me and help me to be at peace. Amen.`

To Be Forgiven, We Must Forgive

"Let all bitterness and wrath and anger and clamor and slander be put away from you, along with all malice. Be kind to one another, tenderhearted, forgiving one another, as God in Christ forgave you" Ephesians 4:31-32.

"And whenever you stand praying, forgive, if you have anything against anyone, so that your Father also who is heaven may forgive you your trespasses," Mark 11:25.

Forgiveness may be the most difficult thing you will ever do if you believe that someone else is to blame for the tragedy. As presented earlier, you now understand that judgment and punishment are not your responsibility. God will take care of that for you. You do not have to be burdened with that. Perhaps you felt some relief about judgment, but you are still troubled because you know that God also expects you to forgive the wrongdoer.

You hear forgiveness discussed in church, and you have read about it in the Scriptures. The verses above instruct Christians to let all bitterness be put away from us. We are not only to avoid thinking about such things; we are to remove these feelings from our heart and mind. It is hard. It may feel impossible. You may have said "I will never forgive the person for that." So, we will take forgiveness in steps. This devotional introduces the reasons we are expected to forgive.

Why must we forgive? We must because Jesus has already forgiven us when we ask Him to do so. If the other person who did the wrongs against you or a family member, has requested forgiveness from God, then they have already been forgiven. If they have not repented, they will be judged in the future. As the verse above from Ephesians states, Christians are to love others and be kind. This means that we cannot continue to wish them harm nor can we continue to harbor anger and bitterness toward them. Why should we forgive others? We must because Jesus has already done this for us. He demonstrated this by giving His life for us.

In the passage from Mark, Jesus reminds us that unless we forgive everyone who may have wronged us, we will not be forgiven. Jesus said if we have anything at all against anyone we must forgive them. That is pretty clear. We cannot forgive those we love and not forgive the one with whom we are angry because of the wrong they committed that caused the tragedy. Forgiveness cannot be selective; we must forgive everyone.

Take some time to think about these verses. The goal at this point in your journey is to introduce these concepts for you to think about. You could probably make a list of all the reasons you can't forgive the person. But there is one reason that you must consider forgiveness. Know this: **Jesus first forgave you and you are redeemed so that you may live more like Christ.** This means forgiving all others as He has forgiven us. Notice the word here, it is important, 'as God has forgiven us.' God does not forgive everyone. God's forgiveness is not given to those who practice malicious, willful sin with no repentance. Therefore, Christians are not required to forgive those who practice malicious, willful sin with no repentance. Such are enemies of God. – Hebrews 10:26-31; Psalm 139:21-22; Proverbs 15:29; 28:9.

Heavenly Father, thank you for giving your Son so that we can be forgiven. Help me to clean my heart so that I may forgive all others that God would also forgive. Amen.

Forgiveness of Others Part 1

"Then Peter came up and said to him, 'Lord, how often will my brother sin against me, and I forgive him? As many as seven times?" Jesus said to him, 'I do not say to you seven times, but seventy times seven.'" Matthew 18: 21-22

"For if you forgive others their trespasses, your heavenly Father will also forgive you, but if you do not forgive others their trespasses, neither will your Father forgive your trespasses" Matthew 6:14-15

Jesus truly emphasized how important forgiveness is in the verse from Matthew 18 above. We are not to forgive others once, not seven times, but 490 times! Jesus was making the point that there is no number when it comes to our forgiving others. And we are talking about forgiving that person, whom you may blame, once! It is clear that the expectations for us to forgive those who sinned against us are tremendous! There is just no getting around it. This may be a stop on your journey that you are not ready for. You can take all the time you need to process these verses and speak to your own heart. No one is rushing you, and it is understandable that this is difficult. Forgiveness is so difficult for some people that it takes years and years until they feel in their heart that they can forgive the wrongdoer.

The second verse from Matthew above is yet another reminder that in order for us to be forgiven, we must first forgive others. Jesus is quite serious about this. We should think about it with great seriousness. Initially, we may have been dismissive about forgiveness of the wrongdoer by simply saying, "I can't do it ever," and left it at that. God expects more, and He knows that, by the fact that you are reading these passages and thinking about forgiveness, you are working on it.

So how do you begin? Read and reread the Scriptures so that the fullness of their meaning and the seriousness with which you must consider forgiveness sinks into your heart and mind. Ask God to help you. When you are praying, ask God to make this something within your grasp. This is part of the test of the tragedy you may not have thought about before. But this is part of the test of your faith and your love for God. Ask Him for knowledge, strength, and compassion for the wrongdoer so that you can prepare yourself for this difficult task.

"Judge not, and you will not be judged; condemn not, and you will not be condemned; forgive, and you will be forgiven" Luke 6:37.

As you think about these passages and pray, know this: **God will provide you with the strength and compassion you need for forgiveness when you ask Him.** And remember, you are on His clock, so this may take longer than you anticipate. But keep praying. Keep trying. You will reach the place you need to go. Remember from the previous devotional that you are not obligated to forgive everyone, such as those who have sinned willfully and still have an unrepentant heart.

Heavenly Father, thank you for forgiving me. Please help me to have compassion for the wrongdoer that is worthy of your forgiveness so that I may follow the example set by Jesus. Amen.

Forgiveness of Others Part 2

"When anyone hears the word of the kingdom and does not understand it, the evil one comes and snatches away what has been sown in his heart. This is what was sown along the path" Matthew 13:19.

"For the mind that is set on the flesh is hostile to God, for it does not submit to God's law; indeed, it cannot" Romans 8:7.

If your tragedy involved the actions of another, those actions might have been purposeful, or they may have been accidental. For example, in a car accident, if the road was wet, the person's brakes failed, and the crash happened, this was not intentional. You may still harbor blame, and you may still need to wrestle with forgiveness. But what if the tragedy of a car accident was caused by road rage? What if it was caused by driving after consuming alcohol? These are actions that were intentional and sinful. What if the tragedy involved a person committing a crime against you or a family member? Or if it was abuse inflicted upon you or a family member? Forgiveness in these situations may truly feel impossible.

The Scripture provides us with some knowledge of how we can reason our way into the act of forgiveness. The first verse above reminds us that when a person does not know about God or Jesus, that person's heart and mind are just waiting to be consumed by sin and sinful actions. In fact, the verse states that sinfulness is what the person has learned rather than learning about God. When a person learns this type of lifestyle, sin will happen. Evil intentions will fill the heart of such a person. The second verse states that when people are only in tune with their own physical wants and desires, they actively reject God. In fact, this verse says it is impossible for this person to behave in a Godly way because they are only concerned with earthly wishes.

You might be saying "What does this have to do with me and forgiving the other person?" Simple. These verses guide us to how we should pray for that person. These individuals have not known God. Their hearts are full of evil intent. Because they have not known God, they reject all manner of godliness and are not living as God expects. So, we pray for them to find God. We pray that they can be turned around. Know this: **God has given us words to help us understand that these individuals need to be brought to Him.** By understanding we are to pray for those who sinned against us, we can move on to forgiveness. You can pray to forgive their sinfulness and pray for their future to be better. Pray that they have a future with God. If you can follow these steps, you can forgive.

Heavenly Father, I have had pain in my heart and have not known how to pray for the wrongdoer. Please help me to forgive them if they are worthy of your forgiveness. Please guide them to seek you. Amen.

Forgiveness of Self

"For all have sinned and fall short of the glory of God and are justified by his grace as a gift through the redemption that is Christ Jesus Romans 3:23-24

There may be some aspects of your past that are associated with the trauma that continue to cause feelings of guilt. This may be that you think the trauma or tragedy was your fault or partially your fault. You may feel responsible for some detail or for some action or inaction. It may be that you have had struggles with your relationships. You may have family or friends with whom you feel you have had harsh words or from whom you have withdrawn. Or maybe it is that you have felt that you have not fulfilled your obligations at work or home since the tragedy. It might be that you continue to neglect your faith life, your church community, or other acts of worship that you participated in actively prior to the tragedy. As the first verse points out, we are all sinners. Of that, there is no question.

You may have had a difficult time forgiving others. If you were able to work through this in the previous devotionals and feel you are now moving forward, that is wonderful, and you can rejoice in these milestones. But you may find that it is more difficult to forgive yourself. Why is this? It is because of that same nemesis: guilt. We have so much trouble turning it over to God. We have a difficult time forgiving ourselves because, for whatever reason, we continue to think we are responsible for our own judgment and our own punishment. Remember this is God's responsibility only and not yours.

When a person absolutely confesses to God, and asks Jesus for forgiveness, and accepts the complete word of God and the resurrection of Jesus as their savior, they can begin anew. This is true for you even if you have been baptized, confirmed, and were an active church member before the tragedy. Until you completely, 100%, turn this over to God, you will continue to carry the weight on your shoulders.

As the verses below tell us, we will be completely clean again. This is the most liberating feeling you can experience after a tragedy. This will provide you with the largest step on your faith journey.

"If we confess our sins, he is faithful and just to forgive us our sins and to cleanse us from all unrighteousness" 1 John 1:9

"There is therefore now no condemnation for those who are in Christ Jesus" Romans 8:1

"Just so, I tell you, there will be more joy in heaven over one sinner who repents than over ninety-nine righteous persons who need no repentance" Luke 15:7

Read the second verse again. There is no condemnation for those who are in Christ. No condemnation. How can you forgive yourself? You must pray. Continue to pray and think about turning it over to Him. Know this: **confessing and accepting Christ again in your life will allow you to move forward in the way nothing else can match.** Close your eyes, pray, confess. Ask forgiveness. And now think this thought: "This is my second chance to live my life and now Christ is with me always." If you are successful in turning this over to God, you will know it. You will feel it. You will be free from the heavy weight. And then you must ask anyone else to whom you feel you have wronged, for their forgiveness if you have not already done so. And in all sins, you, of course, ask God for forgiveness.

If you cannot forgive yourself this at this time, continue to pray, continue to read the Scripture, and return to this devotional and other resources that speak to you about redemption. You will be able to move forward in life with more joy in your heart if you can forgive yourself. As stated before, this does not mean the tragedy is downplayed. It is just in the past. Keep it there.

Heavenly Father, I am sorry for the wrongs I have done, for the sins I have committed. I come to you with humbleness in my heart and ask for forgiveness and to be given a new life in Christ. Amen.

New Life in Christ

"For with the heart one believes and is justified, and with the mouth one confesses and is saved" Romans 10:10

"Therefore, if anyone is in Christ, he is a new creation. The old has passed away; behold, the new has come" 2 Corinthians 5:17

"Jesus answered him, 'Truly, truly, I say to you, unless one is born again, he cannot see the kingdom of God'" John 3:3

You are advancing far along on your journey of faith. If you have been able to complete the last devotional, asking forgiveness, forgiving all others, confessing all sins, you have now been forgiven by the sacrifice that Jesus made for you. You are redeemed by His grace.

Accepting this forgiveness, accepting Jesus to be in your heart and in your life, provides you with a second opportunity to live beyond the tragedy. It is in the past, always, but your burden has been lifted by God's own hand. His fingers reached down and took the burden, the guilt, the shame, the anxiety, sadness, off of your shoulders. The old has passed away. Jesus referred to this freeing feeling as being born again. Why? You feel as though you have been freed because you have started over with a fresh outlook. You now can walk with a brisker step, a bigger smile on your face, and Jesus in your heart. As the Scripture says above, you will be able to see the kingdom of heaven.

When you have reached this part of your journey, you may feel like you want to take off on your own, reading Scripture, going to church again, and enjoying life more. You may feel the Scripture more intently; you may sing the hymns with more enthusiasm, you may want to share your news with everyone that you are once again right with God. Channel that energy into your life. Continue your faith journey by delving deeper into the Bible.

People also find that they look at others with more empathy. Their feelings are restored for things they enjoy in life. Relish every moment and then thank God for the many blessings you have. Offer thanks to God because He did not give up on you. Offer thanks to God for His patience and guidance. Attempt to live in a more Christ-like manner, showing kindness and consideration to others in your life. In the verse below, Paul wrote to the Galatians and explained his own feelings about living with Christ within his heart.

> *"I have been crucified with Christ. It is no longer I who live, but Christ who lives in me. And the life I now live in the flesh I live by faith in the Son of God, who loved me and gave himself for me" Galatians 2:20*

This verse reminds us that now Christ lives in us since we have accepted him. Know this: **being born again in Christ is the greatest freedom you will ever experience and living with Him in your heart will provide you many blessings.** Continue on your journey. Now, rather than walking along the route, you may be skipping along, with God at your side, cheering you on.

Heavenly Father, thank you for giving me a second chance to live in Christ. Please keep me strong and help me to grow my faith. Amen.

Our Expressions of Thankfulness

"Give thanks in all circumstances; for this is the will of God in Christ Jesus for you" 1 Thessalonians 5:18

"Do not be conformed to this world, but be transformed by the renewal of your mind, that by testing you may discern what is the will of God, what is good and acceptable and perfect" Romans 12:2

"Giving thanks always and for everything to God the Father in the name of our Lord Jesus Christ" Ephesians 5:20

You likely have heard all of your life that you should be thankful to God for everything. We give thanks for food, shelter, our jobs, our spouse and family, our friends. We give thanks for the beautiful earth on which we live; we give thanks for opportunities, and all kinds of fun activities and events. We should give thanks often.

But according to the verses above, we should give thanks for everything. This means we should also give thanks for the bad things that happen in our lives. It is even more troubling to think that, according to the first and second Scriptures above, all things are God's will. Does this mean He wants bad things to happen to us? Certainly not. In the devotionals on forgiveness, you learned more about how evil may have interacted with other factors and caused a tragedy. What are we to be thankful for then? What the Scripture is telling us in the second verse is that when we experienced these things, God's will is that we will think about the perfect and good things and discern the best ways for us to respond to these tragedies. The fact that you have read through these devotionals, and you have worked very hard to understand your tragedy and your own faith journey, means you are acting as God wishes you to do. You are looking for the perfect and best ways to work through this journey and to move closer to God.

You may still think about the past events. If you worked through the forgiveness devotionals and you are living your life anew with Christ in your heart, then you have successfully negotiated this very difficult road. It may have taken you a long time to reach this spot in the road. You may still look back. Once in a while, you will feel that sadness, the anxiety. It may be far less than before, but it may return occasionally. Know this: **all the days of your life, you can rely on God for strength and keep His love in your heart, always.** Give thanks to God that you have traveled this far on your journey.

> *"The Lord is my strength and my shield; in him my heart trusts, and I am helped; my heart exults, and with my song I give thanks to him," Psalm 28:7*

Heavenly Father, thank you for loving me and guiding me on my faith journey. Help me to stay near to you. Amen.

God is not Finished Yet

"The apostles said to the Lord, 'Increase our faith'"
Luke 17:5

"No distrust made him waver concerning the promise of God, but he grew strong in his faith as he gave glory to God, fully convinced that God was able to do what he had promised," Romans 4:20-21

"For we walk by faith, not by sight" 2 Corinthians 5:7

"But to all who did receive him, who believed in his name, he gave the right to become the children of God" John 1:12

You have made so much headway on your journey. It has not been easy, and it has not been quick. But, you have more work to do. You may still be excited about your new feelings of freedom and love from God as you have been forgiven and have forgiven others. You may feel less guilt and shame than ever before. This is not the time to slow down on the road. You are not quite to the end yet. And, in fact, you will be traveling the rest of your life as you continue to walk with God. As the first verse above tells us, even the apostles asked to have their faith strengthened. Even the apostles continued to grow their faith! This is a journey that will continue even though you are feeling better about your past. You are now truly considered to be a child of God.

We are told that in order to continue in the way of trust, love, and to make the most of our faith, we must grow our faith. We must strengthen our knowledge of God, our understanding of the Scriptures. We should keep moving closer to God. Faith is very important for us to have and to nurture.

"So faith comes from hearing, and hearing through the word of Christ," Romans 10:17.

"Heaven and earth will pass away, but my words will not pass away" Matthew 24:35

We are told that our faith will increase by hearing the words of Christ. Since the last book of the Bible was completed about 2,000 years ago, it is clear that it has stood the test of time and will continue to be here always. But we should expect no less since this is the word of God. What does God expect from you now? You received Christ, you have begun to live with the tragedy in the background rather than the foreground. But God expects that you will try to understand even more of the Scripture and, more important, live as Christ would expect you to do. He guided you through this difficult time in your life. Know this: **God will be there for you in times of need, and He wants you with Him even when times are good.** Stay with God. Read more Scriptures. Pray more. Give thanks.

"In all your ways acknowledge him, and he will make straight your paths" Proverbs 3:6

Heavenly Father, thank you for being patient with me and loving me always. Please help me to continue to grow in faith and serve you. Amen.

God's Plans for You

"For I know the plans I have for you, declares the Lord, plans for welfare and not for evil, to give you a future and a hope" Jeremiah 29:11

"But, as it is written, 'What no eye has seen, nor ear heard, nor the heart of man imagined, what God has prepared for those who love him'--these things God has revealed to us through the Spirit. For the Spirit searches everything, even the depths of God" 1 Corinthians 2:9-10

Your past experiences were so very difficult. Yet, through the strength provided by God, you have come to this point in your faith journey. You may occasionally have sadness about the past, but you know that God is right beside you and you can lean on His strong shoulder when you need to. He will continue to lift you up. All of this has prepared you for the next steps. You are being prepared for something that you cannot even imagine. God has seen your hard work. He knows you have prayed, forgiven others and yourself, and trusted in His Son. He watched you grow in your faith. He knows you are still walking beside Him and want to learn and read more of His word.

Only God knows the plans He has for you. For those who have faith and believe and follow Him, He promises hope and to assist you with good things happening in your life. Just as you felt the Spirit in your heart, mind, and soul, when you were baptized, it is now growing stronger in you. The Spirit will be with you as you embark on the new era of your life. You will be working on a plan that only God could design.

How will you know what the plan will be? How will you know the direction in which you are to go?

"Your word is a lamp to my feet and a light to my path" Psalm 119:105

"He restores my soul. He leads me in paths of righteousness for his name's sake" Psalm 23:3

"Lead me, O Lord, in your righteousness because of my enemies; make your way straight before me" Psalm 5:8

The Scripture will be your roadmap for this next part of your faith journey. Use the words of God to lead you. Follow the examples of the way Christ lived on earth and how you are to live your life. Know this: **God will lead the way for you, and He will even show you a straight path if you find yourself amongst enemies.** Stay close to Him, and He will be with you.[9]

Heavenly Father, thank you for sending Jesus to set an example of how we are to live. Please guide me in the direction you wish me to go. Amen.

---

[9] HOW TO STUDY YOUR BIBLE: Rightly Handling the Word of God (ISBN-13: 978-1-945757-62-4) http://tiny.cc/px5bty

Witnessing to Others

"As each has received a gift, use it to serve one another, as good stewards of God's varied grace" 1 Peter 4:10

"In all things I have shown you that by working hard in this way we must help the weak and remember the words of the Lord Jesus, how he himself said, 'It is more blessed to give than to receive'" Acts 20:35

"For even the Son of Man came not to be served but to serve, and to give his life as a ransom for many" Mark 10:45

God has given us so many gifts. We should thank Him frequently for the many blessings in our life. If you begin to feel any sadness, regret, guilt, or other negative emotions as you move on this new part of your faith journey, stop and thank God for the blessings you have. This is a good way to stop the negative thought patterns quickly.

As you are now growing stronger in your faith, you are watching as God leads you in the direction in which you need to go next. You have been anticipating the next stop on the road. Where will God take you?

The words from God clearly indicate that we are to use our many blessings. Our gifts have probably helped us along all of our lives. Our gifts are God-given. We should always give God the glory when we have achieved something wonderful in our lives. At this point in your journey, God tells us to share our gifts. We are to use our gifts to help others.

How can you use these gifts?

"In the same way, let your light shine before others, so that they may see your good works and give glory to your Father who is in heaven" Matthew 5:16

Think about serving God by serving others. What gifts do you have from God that you can share? Do you have skills or talents that you can use? How can these gifts be used? Gifts can include having terrific interpersonal skills with people, speaking to groups, teaching, writing, organizing events for charity, assisting in church activities, assisting neighbors and family who need support, holding social events to share fellowship, just to name a few examples. Know this: **Whatever you do for God, you will reap your rewards in heaven.** By living in this manner, you are serving to witness to others that your own faith guides your life. This will serve to teach others how those in Christ live and help others.

You have suffered a trauma that was life-changing. Others have, too. If it is at all possible, help those individuals move forward in their journey. This is a wonderful way to serve.[10]

Heavenly Father, thank you for the gifts and blessings you have given me. Please use me as your servant. Amen.

---

[10] Resources for witnessing to others: http://tiny.cc/fl5bty

Holding on Tightly to God's Hand

"No temptation has overtaken you that is not common to man. God is faithful, and he will not let you be tempted beyond your ability, but with the temptation he will also provide the way of escape, that you may be able to endure it" 1 Corinthians 10:13

"Like newborn infants, long for the pure spiritual milk, that by it you may grow up into salvation" 1 Peter 2:2

Your life is probably flowing into a new routine. You have overcome so much and expanded your faith along the way. You may have days when things are going so smoothly that you slip away from God. You may have times when you are involved in your work, family, and other activities, that you put God on the backburner. Perhaps you are not scheduling time to include reading Scripture and devotionals. Maybe you do not feel that you need God as much now. This happens to us all. If this continues and your heart and mind become more accustomed to the worldly concerns, you may also slip back into negative thought patterns. Remember that holding tightly to God's hand in your typical day will strengthen you. Reading the Scripture with attentiveness will help provide you with the strength you need.

You well know, through your own travel on your faith journey, that God is patient. He has waited for you to make this trip and He continues to be right beside you. He is faithful to you even when you may not be faithful to Him. The first verse tells us that falling away from God, and other actions that are tempting to us are not uncommon. In His steadfast faithfulness to us, He is making certain that any temptations you might have are countered by the strength and ability He has given to you. The strength and wisdom you have are enough to avoid the temptations or to endure these temptations. This can include the temptations of falling back into negative thinking about yourself or others.

The second verse notes that, like infants, we must continue to search for and acquire knowledge from the Scripture if we are to obtain salvation and a full life in Christ. By relying on God always, He will be there when we need Him next.

"And call upon me in the day of trouble; I will deliver you, and you shall glorify me" Psalm 50:15

"Therefore, brothers, be all the more diligent to make your calling and election sure, for if you practice these qualities, you will never fall. For in this way there will be richly provided for you an entrance into the eternal kingdom of our Lord and Savior Jesus Christ" 2 Peter 1:10-11

Should you be tempted or fall away from God, ask Him for help. You know He will help you. Try, as hard as you can, to be consistent with your faith. By this practice, you will not fall. Know this: **God wants your faith to continue and will provide you with the strength and guidance to do so but He also wants you to ask for help when you fall away.** Because the Bible is the word of God, God is readily available to you at all times. Read the passages, pray, and be thankful for your faith.

Heavenly Father, thank you for helping me so much in my times of need. Forgive me when I do not pay attention to my faith. Guide me back to you. Amen.

Rejoicing in the Light

"Rejoice in the Lord always; again I say, rejoice"
Philippians 4:4

"This is the day that the Lord has made; let us rejoice and be glad in it" Psalm 118:24

"May the God of hope fill you with all joy and peace in believing, so that by the power of the Holy Spirit you may abound in hope" Romans 15:13

Rejoice that you have continued on this difficult journey. Rejoice that you have been able to forgive others and yourself. Be thankful that God has given you such strength and endurance to get through to this side of your tragedy. You are truly blessed. Be thankful for each blessing you have seen along the way.

Each morning, you can give thanks to God for bringing you another day in which you can love and serve God. Although you may have daily stresses of work and family life, rejoice in every minute of the day. Look at the blessings you have.

As the Bible tells us, joy and peace are yours because you believe. Your beliefs are held in your heart and have been growing thanks to the Holy Spirit. Be thankful that your heart has been opened to the Holy Spirit and that you are staying near to God.

"The Lord your God is in your midst, a mighty one who will save; he will rejoice over you with gladness; he will quiet you by his love; he will exult over you with loud singing" Zephaniah 3:17

"I have no greater joy than to hear that my children are walking in the truth" 3 John 1:4

Because you continue to walk with God, He is rejoicing for you! You are walking in the truth just as the followers in the Bible did. You have found your faith again or perhaps for the first time. This means that your life has changed for the better even though you had an experience in the past that was tragic. You can now rejoice that God will take care of you and has brought you through this journey to the other side where you can rejoice and share your faith by example. Share your faith by serving others. Know this: **As you rejoice in God's love, He is rejoicing that you are walking in the light and the truth with Him.**

> *"But let all who take refuge in you rejoice; let them ever sing for joy, and spread your protection over them, that those who love your name may exult in you"* Psalm 5:11

Heavenly Father, I praise you for your love and devotion to me. Thank you for my many blessings. Strengthen me to always walk with you. Amen.

Moving Beyond

"Do not neglect to do good and to share what you have, for such sacrifices are pleasing to God" Hebrews 13:16

"Let each of you look not only to his own interests, but also to the interests of others" Philippians 2:4

"Do not withhold good from those to whom it is due, when it is in your power to do it" Proverbs 3:27

Congratulations on the progress you have made. You are now ready to truly become more engrossed in the word of God, to serve others, and work as you know Christ would want you to do. You have read that you are to share your own gifts and talents. You know that one way to serve is to help others who have been through tragedies like you have suffered.

For the readers of this book, my prayers are with you. It has been my goal to write this devotional for you so that I can serve God and be a witness to you of His strong and patient love. He has worked in us so that we may now bring glory to Him.

As a traveler on my own journey, I know that the road has not ended for me and it will not end soon for you. God has plans for us all. We are to watch for His guidance, ask for help, and continue down the path. I hope your journey did not take as many years as mine. Speaking from experience, there may still be rough days. When you encounter such times, take a moment, take a deep breath, read your favorite passages that give you strength. Help others when you can, this will serve to lift you up. Should you feel you are slipping back further on your journey, that perhaps you made a U-turn and drove the wrong way on the road, open this book up again, take the assessment and see where you are. Once you determine where you are in your journey, refer to the pages in the devotional to help you move forward again.

God is patient and has waited for you to make the journey to this point. Take His hand and walk along beside Him again. Know this: **Through all the tests and trials of life, God will give you strength** and He has a plan to make all of the bad events of life weave into something good.

Heavenly Father, I pray that you will continue to help me grow in my faith and service to you. Thank you for the many blessings you have given to me and for the strength you have provided to me to make this journey. Amen.

APPENDIX 1 Where Are You in Your Own Journey?

This self-assessment is provided to assist you in determining where you might be in your own faith journey. Each person follows their own path designed by God at His pace. This assessment may help you to determine that there are next steps that will bring you ever closer to Christ and to re-establish your faith if you feel it has weakened due to the crisis. Read each item and check the statement that best describes how you feel at this moment. Follow the instructions after the assessment to help determine where you might be on your journey. Once you have completed the scoring of the assessment, turn to the first devotional and begin your faith journey.

1. When thinking about the trauma or crisis that happened to me or in my family, I:

    ____ a. Think there is some mistake, this crisis did not happen

    ____ b. Think the crisis should be hidden and never acknowledged

    ____ c. Think the crisis has brought me closer to God

    ____ d. Think the crisis has enabled me to witness to others or better serve Christ

2. When thinking about the trauma or crisis that happened, I:

    ____ a. Know that the perpetrator or other events that happened are to blame

    ____ b. Blame a family member or another person and perhaps myself

    ____ c. Blame myself

    ____ d. Acknowledge that this was the work of evil in a person or evil in the world or events out of my control

3. I would describe my heart or emotions as:

    ____ a. Dead inside

_____ b. Angry

_____ c. Sad, depressed, gloomy

_____ d. Loving and warm

4. As far as I am concerned:

_____ a. There is no God or, if there is, He is not for me

_____ b. God exists but I do not have faith in Him anymore

_____ c. God exists and I pray sometimes

_____ d. God and His Son, Jesus Christ, provided me guidance during this test

5. I know that:

_____ a. I will never forgive the individual(s) that inflicted this pain or trauma

_____ b. I will try as hard as I can to see that this person or persons are punished

_____ c. It is not up to me to see that others are punished

_____ d. God will judge everyone, and if punishment is due, it will be rendered

6. When thinking about the trauma or crisis:

_____ a. I know that I deserved this to happen to me

_____ b. I know that this was not deserved and I harbor anger

_____ c. I know that evil exists in the world and there are some events that cannot be controlled

_____ d. I know that in God's time the significance of this will be revealed to me in His plan

7. When thinking about the trauma or crisis:

_____ a. I realize the best thing for me to do is distance myself from everyone

_____ b. I know that something I plan to do in the future will make me happier

_____ c. I know that I am getting closer to being happier

_____ d. I know that I have complete contentment through Jesus Christ's redemption

8. When thinking about the trauma or crisis:

_____ a. I am very depressed

_____ b. I feel numb, but I am able to go through the everyday motions of life

_____ c. I no longer think about it, it is in a mental "box" or compartment in my mind or pretend it never happened

_____ d. I know that evil caused this to happen, or other events are not in my control, and my faith keeps me strong

9. When thinking about my reaction to the trauma or crisis:

_____ a. I cannot think about it, I am too upset

_____ b. I choose not to think about it, I ignore those thoughts or put them away

_____ c. I am able to go on with my day-to-day life in a productive manner

_____ d. I know that my heart and soul have been cleansed and my life is good thanks to God

10. When I think about God:

_____ a. I no longer have faith in God

_____ b. I sometimes try to believe in God

_____ c. I believe in God the Father, His Son Jesus, and the Holy Spirit

_____ d. I feel completely forgiven or redeemed, I have a new life in Jesus Christ

11. When I think about my journey:

_____ a. I feel I am stuck

_____ b. I feel that I have moved forward but then I move backward again

_____ c. I have made progress and I am moving closer to forgiveness and contentment

_____ d. I have struggled, but now I know God's purpose for this crisis in my life

12. When I think about my journey:

_____ a. I hope I can move forward someday

_____ b. I am thinking about reading the Bible or seeking help from others in the church or through counseling

_____ c. I read the Bible or devotionals frequently or attend church and try to strengthen my faith

_____ d. I now know that God's plan includes serving others in some capacity

To get a better idea of where you might be in your faith journey, add the points as instructed below:

a. = 1 point each

b. = 2 points each

c. = 3 points each

d. = 4 points each

Total of a. = _____

Total of b. = _____

Total of c. = _____

Total of d.= _____

Total of all= _____

Total of 12-20- You may just be starting your faith journey. For individuals who feel a high level of depression, please ask your pastor, or others in the church or community, to assist you in finding support such as counseling. Pray, read Scripture, talk to your pastor and others in the church who can help you on your faith journey.

Total of 21-32-You are moving along in your faith journey. Continue to move forward by talking with those who support you, reading the Bible, reading devotionals, praying, working on projects with others in the community or in church.

Total of 33-40-You are making great progress in your faith journey. Continue to move forward and consider how you might be of service to those in the church or other areas. Continue to read the Bible, praying, reading devotionals, and serving others.

Total of 41-48-You are reaching a great place in your faith journey as you depend on God to help you see His plan for you. Continue to be involved with prayer, Scripture, and the church. Continue to serve others.

APPENDIX 2 My Faith Journey

1-----→	2-----→	3-----→	4
Life Before Event	Event	Shock And Disbelief Rejection Of God A Quick Fix	Deep Depression Searching For Happiness
5-----→	**6-----→**	**7-----→**	**8-----→**
God Exists For Others Searching For Happiness	God Exists But Still Angry At God Searching For Happiness Connecting With Others	Anniversaries Awareness Of God's Presence For Me Searching For Happiness	Turning Judgment Over To God
9-----→	**10-----→**	**11-----→**	**12-----→**
Forgiveness Of Others	Forgiveness Of Self	New Life In Christ	Witness To Others Rejoice In the Light Moving Beyond

1. Life Before Event- Everything seemed normal. Life is good.

2. Event- This may be the actual occurrence of the event or your first knowledge of the event (as in a disclosure of an event in the past)

3. Shock and Disbelief and Rejection of God-There is so much shock that the reaction is anger and rejection of God for allowing this to happen. You may look for a quick solution to make things better or to make things right, back to "normal" before the event. You may feel helpless like nothing can be done to make things better.

4. Deep Depression-This is a time to seek help of some kind whether this is through counseling, a pastor, friends, or family to support all involved. You may feel that no one can ever understand what you have been through. You may also find yourself searching but you do not know what you are

searching for. This might mean moving, changing jobs, or other significant activities to try, without success, to find happiness.

5. <u>God Exists for Others</u>-There can be no denying God. For those who are already Christians, the Spirit is already within and is waiting for the right time. This may take a while to resolve the anger and hurt. You may still find yourself searching. You may be able to acknowledge there is a God, but He is for other people, not you.

6. <u>God Exists But Still Angry at God</u>-There may be some acknowledgment that God exists and is involved in your life but there may continue to be a lack of trust. Your relationship with God is still shaky. You may continue to search for answers, happiness, or solutions. You may Question if it is OK to be happy. You may begin to reconnect with others.

7. <u>Awareness of God's Presence for Me</u>-Although acknowledgment of God has occurred, there may still be reluctance in understanding or believing that God forgives all sinners who ask or there may be some reluctance in totally trusting God and forgiving others. You may continue to search. You may have difficulty with anniversary dates and celebrations.

8. <u>Turning Judgement Over to God</u>-This is the time of realization that judgment and any possible punishment that may be due is not up to anyone except God. Many verses in the Bible direct us to leave this to God.

9. <u>Forgiveness of Others</u>-This is a step that you may never think you can do. It is very difficult to do right away and God will lead you to the direction you need to take by reading Bible verses and consulting with your pastor or listening to fellow Christians. It is an amazing step to achieve and will bound you forward to healing.

10. <u>Forgiveness of Self</u>- This step is difficult but very freeing. You may have already been able to forgive others. Your journey may involve forgiving other people or only forgiving yourself for any blame you may have assigned to yourself.

11. <u>New Life in Christ</u>- This is the most freeing. Reaching this step provides a sense of starting completely over; everything feels new. and everything feels free from blame, sin, anger.

12. <u>Witness to Others</u> – As part of your new Christian life, you may feel the sudden desire to help others or to be in service to God. No matter how this is manifested in your life, you will see the new purpose for you, and you will be able to see that some good can come from tragedies.

APPENDIX 3 Relationship of Anxiety, Worry, Guilt, and Shame

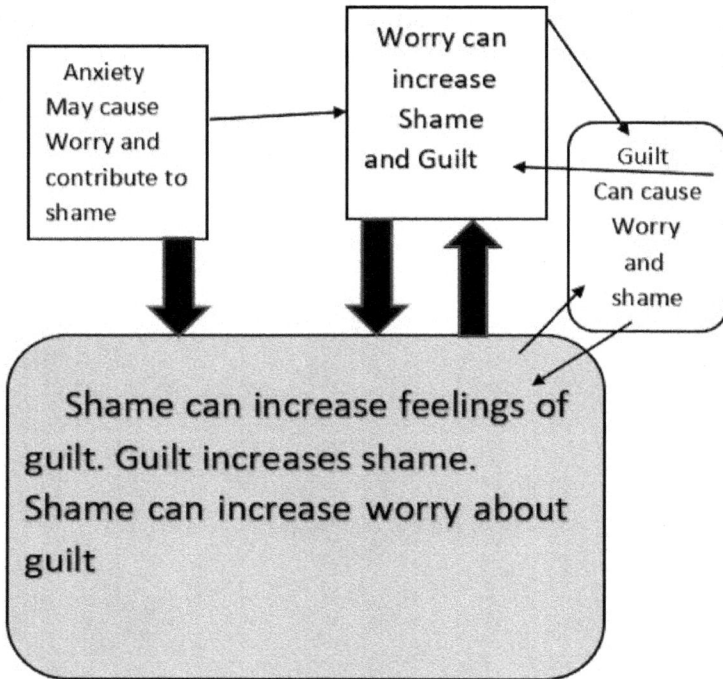

Anxiety
May cause
Worry and
contribute to
shame

Worry can
increase
Shame
and Guilt

Guilt
Can cause
Worry
and
shame

Shame can increase feelings of guilt. Guilt increases shame. Shame can increase worry about guilt

APPENDIX 4

Bible Verses by Devotional Topic

Introductory Passage

"If any of you lacks wisdom, let him ask God, who gives generously to all without reproach, and it will be given him" James 1:5

Before the Tragedy

"Delight yourself in the Lord, and he will give you the desires of your heart" Psalm 37: 4.

"Therefore, since we have been justified by faith, we have peace with God through our Lord Jesus Christ. Through him we have also obtained access by faith into this grace in which we stand, and we rejoice in the hope of the glory of God. More than that, we rejoice in our sufferings, knowing that suffering produces endurance, and endurance produces character, and character produces hope, and hope does not put us to shame, because God's love has been poured into our hearts through the Holy Spirit who has been given to us." Romans 5: 1-5

Trauma or Event

"Beloved, do not be surprised at the fiery trial when it comes upon you to test you, as though something strange were happening to you." 1 Peter 4:12

"It is good that one should wait quietly for the salvation of the Lord" Lamentations 3:26

"Do not fear what you are about to suffer. Behold, the devil is about to throw some of you into prison, that you may be tested..." Revelation 2:10

"And when the Lord saw her, he had compassion on her and said to her, 'Do not weep'" Luke 7:13

Disbelief

"For still the vision awaits its appointed time; it hastens to the end-it will not lie. If it seems slow, wait for it; it will surely come; it will not delay" Habakkuk 2:3

"Be still, and know that I am God..." Psalm 46:10

Rejection of God

"The fool says in his heart, 'there is no God.'" Psalm 14:1

"It is good for me that I was afflicted, that I might learn your statutes" Psalm 119:71

"Jesus answered him, "What I am doing you do not understand now, but afterward you will understand" John 13:7.

"Wait for the Lord; be strong, and let your heart take courage; wait for the Lord!" Psalm 27:14

"Be sober-minded; be watchful. Your adversary the devil prowls around like a roaring lion, seeking someone to devour" 1 Peter 5:8

"And I will give you a new heart, and a new spirit I will put within you. And I will remove the heart of stone from your flesh and give you a heart of flesh". Ezekiel 36:26

A Quick Fix

"Many are the plans in the mind of a man, but it is the purpose of the Lord that will stand" Proverbs 19:21

"And my God will supply every need of yours according to his riches in glory in Christ Jesus" Philippians 4:19

Depression and Sadness

"A man's spirit will endure sickness, but a crushed spirit who can bear?" Proverbs 18:14

"The Lord is near to the brokenhearted and saves the crushed in spirit." Psalm 34:18

"Answer me quickly, O Lord! My spirit fails! Hide not your face from me, lest I be like those who go down to the pit." Psalm 143:7

"You hold my eyelids open; I am so troubled that I cannot speak" Psalm 77:4

"Likewise the Spirit helps us in our weakness. For we do not know what to pray for as we ought, but the Spirit himself intercedes for us with groanings too deep for words" Romans 8:26

"Therefore encourage one another and build one another up, just as you are doing" 1 Thessalonians 5:11

"Truly I say to you, as you did it to one of the least of these my brothers, you did it to me," Matthew 25:40

"Let your eyes look directly forward, and your gaze be straight before you. Ponder the path of your feet; then all your ways will be sure. Do not swerve to the right or to the left; turn your foot away from evil" Proverbs 4: 25-27

Blame

"I have said these things to you, that in me you may have peace. In the world you will have tribulation. But take heart; I have overcome the world" John 16:33.

"So then each of us will give an account of himself to God" Romans 14:12

"Draw near to God, and he will draw near to you..." James 4:8

"The Lord is near to all who call on him, to all who call on him in truth" Psalm 145:18

Anxiety and Worry

"Therefore do not be anxious about tomorrow, for tomorrow will be anxious for itself. Sufficient for the day is its own trouble" Matthew 6:34

"Anxiety in a man's heart weights him down, but a good word makes him glad" Proverbs 12:25

"I can do all things through Him who strengthens me" Philippians 4:13.

"But Jesus looked at them and said, "With man this is impossible, but with God all things are possible" Matthew 19:26

Guilt

"Therefore, since we have been justified by faith, we have peace with God through our Lord Jesus Christ" Romans 5:1

"Casting all your anxieties on him, because he cares for you" 1 Peter 5:7

"Cast your burden on the Lord, and he will sustain you; he will never permit the righteous to be moved" Psalm 55:22

"The Lord upholds all who are falling and raises up all who are bowed down" Psalm 145:14

Shame

"But the Lord God helps me; therefore I have not been disgraced; therefore I have set my face like a flint, and I know that I shall not be put to shame" Isaiah 50:7

"I sought the Lord, and he answered me and delivered me from all my fears. Those who look to him are radiant, and their faces shall never be ashamed" Psalm 34: 4-5

"For the Scripture says, 'Everyone who believes in him will not be put to shame'" Romans 10:11

"But you, O Lord, are a shield about me, my glory, and the lifter of my head" Psalm 3:3

Relationship of Anxiety, Worry, Guilt, and Shame

"For God gave us a spirit not of fear but of power and love and self-control" 2 Timothy 1:7.

"Peace I leave with you; my peace I give you. Not as the world gives do I give to you. Let not your hearts be troubled, neither let them be afraid" John 14:27.

"I sought the Lord and he answered me and delivered me from all my fears" Psalm 34:4

Awareness of God and Residual Anger

"They are darkened in their understanding, alienated from the life of God because of the ignorance that is in them, due to their hardness of heart" Ephesians 4:18

"And how from childhood you have been acquainted with the sacred writings, which are able to make you wise for salvation through faith in Christ Jesus" 2 Timothy 3:15

"He saved us, not because of works done by us in righteousness, but according to his own mercy, by the washing of regeneration and renewal of the Holy Spirit" Titus 3:5

Searching for Happiness

"For everyone who asks receives, and the one who seeks finds, and to the one who knocks it will be opened" Matthew 7:8

"But seek first the kingdom of God and his righteousness, and all these things will be added to you" Matthew 6:33

"I love those who love me, and those who seek me diligently find me" Proverbs 8:17

Moving on from Shame and Guilt

"The thief comes only to steal and kill and destroy. I came that they may have life and have it abundantly" John 10:10

"Look at the birds of the air: they neither sow nor reap nor gather into barns, and yet your heavenly Father feeds them. Are you not of more value than they? Matthew 6:26

"If we confess our sins, he is faithful and just to forgive us our sins and to cleanse us from all unrighteousness" 1 John 1:9

Isolation

"Whoever isolates himself seeks his own desire; he breaks out against all sound judgement" Proverbs 18:1

"By this we know that we abide in him and he in us, because he has given us of his Spirit" 1 John 4:13

"It is the Lord who goes before you. He will be with you; he will not leave you or forsake you. Do not fear or be dismayed" Deuteronomy 31: 8

Seeking Others

"Two are better than one, because they have a good reward for their toil. For if they fall, one will lift up his fellow. But woe to him

who is alone when he falls and has not another to lift him up!" Ecclesiastes 4:9

"That is, that we may be mutually encouraged by each other's faith, both yours and mine" Romans 1:12

"Bear one another's burdens, and so fulfill the law of Christ" Galatians 6:2

Allowing Others in Your Life

"This is my commandment, that you love one another as I have loved you" John 15:12

"Give, and it will be given to you. Good measure, pressed down, shaken together, running over, will be put into your lap. For with the measure you use it will be measured back to you" Luke 6:38

"'The second is this: You shall love your neighbor as yourself.' There is no other commandment greater than these" Mark 12:31

Anniversaries and Other Reminders

"Blessed are those who mourn, for they shall be comforted" Matthew 5:4

"For everything there is a season, and a time for every matter under heaven: a time to be born, and a time to die; a time plant, and to pluck up what is planted; a time to kill, and a time to heal; a time to break down, and a time to build up, a time to weep, and a time to laugh; a time to mourn, and a time to dance..." Ecclesiastes 3: 1-4

"He heals the broken hearted and binds up their wounds" Psalm 147:3

Is It OK to be Happy?

"Even in laughter the heart may ache, and the end of joy may be grief" Proverbs 14:13

"A joyful heart is good medicine, but a crushed spirit dries up the bones" Proverbs 17:22

"Also that everyone should eat and drink and take pleasure in all his toll-this is God's gift to man" Ecclesiastes 3:13

"Then our mouth was filled with laughter, and our tongue with shouts of joy; then they said among the nations, 'The Lord has done great things for them'" Psalm 126:2

Unexpected Reminders

"Keep me as the apple of your eye; hide me in the shadow of your wings" Psalm 17:8

"But the Lord is faithful. He will establish you and guard you against the evil one" 2 Thessalonians 3:3

"Though I walk in the midst of trouble, you preserve my life; you stretch out your hand against the wrath of my enemies, and your right hand delivers me" Psalm 138:7

"The name of the Lord is a strong tower; the righteous man runs into it and is safe" Proverbs 18:10

Stress in Relationships

"My inward parts are in turmoil and never still; days of affliction come to meet me" Job 30:27

"Be angry and do not sin; do not let the sun go down on your anger" Ephesians 4:26

"The Lord will fight for you, and you have only to be silent" Exodus 14:14

"When the cares of my heart are many, your consolations cheer my soul" Psalm 94:19

"I have set the Lord always before me; because he is at my right hand, I shall not be shaken" Psalm 16:8

Questions from Others

"Do not be overcome by evil, but overcome evil with good" Romans 12:21

"A soft answer turns away wrath, but a harsh word stirs up anger" Proverbs 15:1

"But I say to you, love your enemies and pray for those who persecute you" Matthew 5:44

"Let the words of my mouth and the mediation of my heart be acceptable in your sight, O Lord, my rock and my redeemer" Psalm 19:14

"Love one another with brotherly affection. Outdo one another in showing honor" Romans 12:10

Why?

"Count it all joy, my brothers, when you meet trials of various kinds, for you know that the testing of your faith produces steadfastness. And let steadfastness have its full effect, that you may be perfect and complete, lacking nothing" James 1:2-4

"And we know that for those who love God all things work together for good, for those who are called according to his purpose" Romans 8:28

"Blessed is the man who remains steadfast under trial, for when he has stood the test he will receive the crown of life, which God has promised to those who love him" James 1:12

"Rejoice in hope, be patient in tribulation, be constant in prayer" Romans 12:12

Awareness of God's Presence

"You make known to me the path of life; in your presence there is fullness of joy; at your right hand are pleasures forevermore" Psalm 16:11

"May the God of hope fill you with all joy and peace in believing, so that by the power of the Holy Spirit you may abound in hope" Romans 15:13

"Then he opened their minds to understand the Scriptures" Luke 24:45

"Every word of God proves true; he is a shield to those who take refuge in him" Proverbs 30:5

Awareness of God's Presence in My Life

"Now faith is the assurance of things hoped for, the conviction of things not seen. For by it the people of old received their

commendation. By faith we understand that the universe was created by the word of God, so that what is seen was not made out of things that are visible" Hebrews 11: 1-3

"Jesus said to him, 'Have you believed because you have seen me? Blessed are those who have not seen and yet have believed'" John 20:29

"For by grace you have been saved through faith. And this is not your own doing; it is the gift of God" Ephesians 2:8

It's Never Going to Be OK

"So we can confidently say, 'The Lord is my helper; I will not fear; what can man do to me?" Hebrews 13:6

"And give no opportunity to the devil" Ephesians 4:27

"It does not rejoice at wrongdoing, but rejoices with the truth" 1 Corinthians 13: 6

"No man shall be able to stand before you all the days of your life. Just as I was with Moses, so I will be with you. I will not leave you or forsake you" Joshua 1:5

Judgement

"For the wrongdoer will be paid back for the wrong he has done, and there is no partiality" Colossians 3:25

"For we must all appear before the judgement seat of Christ, so that each one may receive what is due for what he has done in the body, whether good or evil" 2 Corinthians 5:10

"Beloved, never avenge yourselves, but leave it to the wrath of God, for it is written, 'Vengeance is mine, I will repay, says the Lord'" Romans 12:19

"Do not say 'I will repay evil'; wait for the Lord, and he will deliver you" Proverbs 20:22.

Forgiveness

"Let all bitterness and wrath and anger and clamor and slander be put away from you, along with all malice. Be kind to one another, tenderhearted, forgiving one another, as God in Christ forgave you" Ephesians 4:31-32.

"And whenever you stand praying, forgive, if you have anything against anyone, so that your Father also who is heaven may forgive you your trespasses," Mark 11:25.

Forgiveness of Others Part 1

"Then Peter came up and said to him, "Lord, how often will my brother sin against me, and I forgive him? As many as seven times?" Jesus said to him, 'I do not say to you seven times, but seventy times seven.'" Matthew 18: 21-22

"For if you forgive others their trespasses, your heavenly Father will also forgive you, but if you do not forgive others their trespasses, neither will your Father forgive your trespasses" Matthew 6:14-15

"Judge not, and you will not be judged; condemn not, and you will not be condemned; forgive, and you will be forgiven" Luke 6:37

Forgiveness of Others Part 2

"When anyone hears the word of the kingdom and does not understand it, the evil one comes and snatches away what has been sown in his heart. This is what was sown along the path" Matthew 13:19.

"For the mind that is set on the flesh is hostile to God, for it does not submit to God's law; indeed, it cannot" Romans 8:7.

Forgiveness of Self

"For all have sinned and fall short of the glory of God and are justified by his grace as a gift through the redemption that is Christ Jesus Romans 3:23-24

"If we confess our sins, he is faithful and just to forgive us our sins and to cleanse us from all unrighteousness" 1 John 1:9

"There is therefore now no condemnation for those who are in Christ Jesus" Romans 8:1

"Just so, I tell you, there will be more joy in heaven over one sinner who repents than over ninety-nine righteous persons who need no repentance" Luke 15:7

A New Life in Christ

"For with the heart one believes and is justified, and with the mouth one confesses and is saved" Romans 10:10

"Therefore, if anyone is in Christ, he is a new creation. The old has passed away; behold, the new has come" 2 Corinthians 5:17

"Jesus answered him, 'Truly, truly, I say to you, unless one is born again, he cannot see the kingdom of God'" John 3:3

"I have been crucified with Christ. It is no longer I who live, but Christ who lives in me. And the life I now live in the flesh I live by faith in the Son of God, who loved me and gave himself for me" Galatians 2:20

Thankfulness

"Give thanks in all circumstances; for this is the will of God in Christ Jesus for you" 1 Thessalonians 5:18

"Do not be conformed to this world, but be transformed by the renewal of your mind, that by testing you may discern what is the will of God, what is good and acceptable and perfect" Romans 12:2

"Giving thanks always and for everything to God the Father in the name of our Lord Jesus Christ" Ephesians 5:20

"The Lord is my strength and my shield; in him my heart trusts, and I am helped; my heart exults, and with my song I give thanks to him, " Psalm 28:7

God Is Not Finished Yet

"The apostles said to the Lord, 'Increase our faith'" Luke 17:5

"No distrust made him waver concerning the promise of God, but he grew strong in his faith as he gave glory to God, fully convinced that God was able to do what he had promised, " Romans 4:20-21

"For we walk by faith, not by sight" 2 Corinthians 5:7

"But to all who did receive him, who believed in his name, he gave the right to become the children of God" John 1:12

"So faith comes from hearing, and hearing through the word of Christ," Romans 10:17.

"Heaven and earth will pass away, but my words will not pass away" Matthew 24:35

"In all your ways acknowledge him, and he will make straight your paths" Proverbs 3:6

God's Plans for You

"For I know the plans I have for you, declares the Lord, plans for welfare and not for evil, to give you a future and a hope" Jeremiah 29:11

"But, as it is written, 'What no eye has seen, nor ear heard, nor the heart of man imagined, what God has prepared for those who love him'--these things God has revealed to us through the Spirit. For the Spirit searches everything, even the depths of God" 1 Corinthians 2:9-10

"Your word is a lamp to my feet and a light to my path" Psalm 119:105

"He restores my soul. He leads me in paths of righteousness for his name's sake" Psalm 23:3

"Lead me, O Lord, in your righteousness because of my enemies; make your way straight before me" Psalm 5:8

Witnessing to Others

"As each has received a gift, use it to serve one another, as good stewards of God's varied grace" 1 Peter 4:10

"In all things I have shown you that by working hard in this way we must help the weak and remember the words of the Lord Jesus, how he himself said, 'It is more blessed to give than to receive'" Acts 20:35

"For even the Son of Man came not to be served but to serve, and to give his life as a ransom for many" Mark 10:45

"In the same way, let your light shine before others, so that they may see your good works and give glory to your Father who is in heaven" Matthew 5:16

Holding on Tightly to God's Hand

"No temptation has overtaken you that is not common to man. God is faithful, and he will not let you be tempted beyond your ability, but with the temptation he will also provide the way of escape, that you may be able to endure it" 1 Corinthians 10:13

"Like newborn infants, long for the pure spiritual milk, that by it you may grow up into salvation" 1 Peter 2:2

"And call upon me in the day of trouble; I will deliver you, and you shall glorify me" Psalm 50:15

"Therefore, brothers, be all the more diligent to make your calling and election sure, for if you practice these qualities, you will never fall. For in this way there will be richly provided for you an entrance into the eternal kingdom of our Lord and Savior Jesus Christ" 2 Peter 1:10-11

Rejoicing in the Light

"Rejoice in the Lord always; again I say, rejoice" Philippians 4:4

"This is the day that the Lord has made; let us rejoice and be glad in it" Psalm 118:24

"May the God of hope fill you with all joy and peace in believing, so that by the power of the Holy Spirit you may abound in hope" Romans 15:13

"The Lord your God is in your midst, a mighty one who will save; he will rejoice over you with gladness; he will quiet you by his love; he will exult over you with loud singing" Zephaniah 3:17

"I have no greater joy than to hear that my children are walking in the truth" 3 John 1:4

"But let all who take refuge in you rejoice; let them ever sing for joy, and spread your protection over them, that those who love your name may exult in you" Psalm 5:11

Moving Beyond

"Do not neglect to do good and to share what you have, for such sacrifices are pleasing to God" Hebrews 13:16

"Let each of you look not only to his own interests, but also to the interests of others" Philippians 2:4

"Do not withhold good from those to whom it is due, when it is in your power to do it" Proverbs 3:27

OTHER RELEVANT BOOKS

"*Rejoice, young person, while you are young, and let your heart be glad in the days of your youth.*"
Wise King Solomon

DEVOTIONAL FOR YOUTHS
GROWING UP IN CHRIST

Terry Overton

Christian Publishing House
ISBN-13: 978-1-945757-90-7
ISBN-10: 1-945757-90-6

"ALL SCRIPTURE IS INSPIRED BY GOD AND PROFITABLE FOR TEACHING, FOR REPROOF, FOR CORRECTION, FOR TRAINING IN RIGHTEOUSNESS"—2 TIMOTHY 3:16

REASONABLE
FAITH

Saving Those Who Doubt

EDWARD D. ANDREWS

Christian Publishing House

ISBN-13: 978-1-945757-91-4

ISBN-10: 1-945757-91-4

Heather Freeman &
Edward D. Andrews

THIRTEEN
REASONS WHY
YOU SHOULD
KEEP LIVING

When Hope and
Love Vanish?

Christian Publishing House

ISBN-13: 978-1-945757-47-1

ISBN-10: 1-945757-47-7

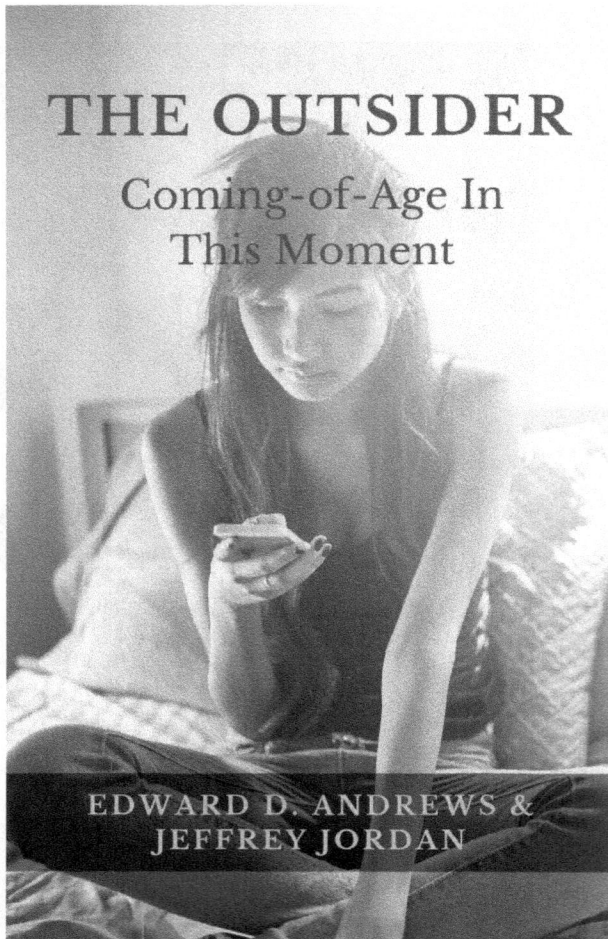

THE OUTSIDER
Coming-of-Age In This Moment

EDWARD D. ANDREWS &
JEFFREY JORDAN

Christian Publishing House

ISBN-13: 978-1-945757-60-0
ISBN-10: 1-945757-60-4

For I delight in the law of God, in my inner being, but I see in my members another law waging war against the law of my mind and making me captive to the law of sin that dwells in my members.—The Apostle Paul (Rom. 7:22-23)

WAGING WAR

A Christian's Cognitive Behavioral Therapy Workbook

Heather Freeman

Christian Publishing House

ISBN-13: 978-1-945757-42-6

ISBN-10: 1-945757-42-6

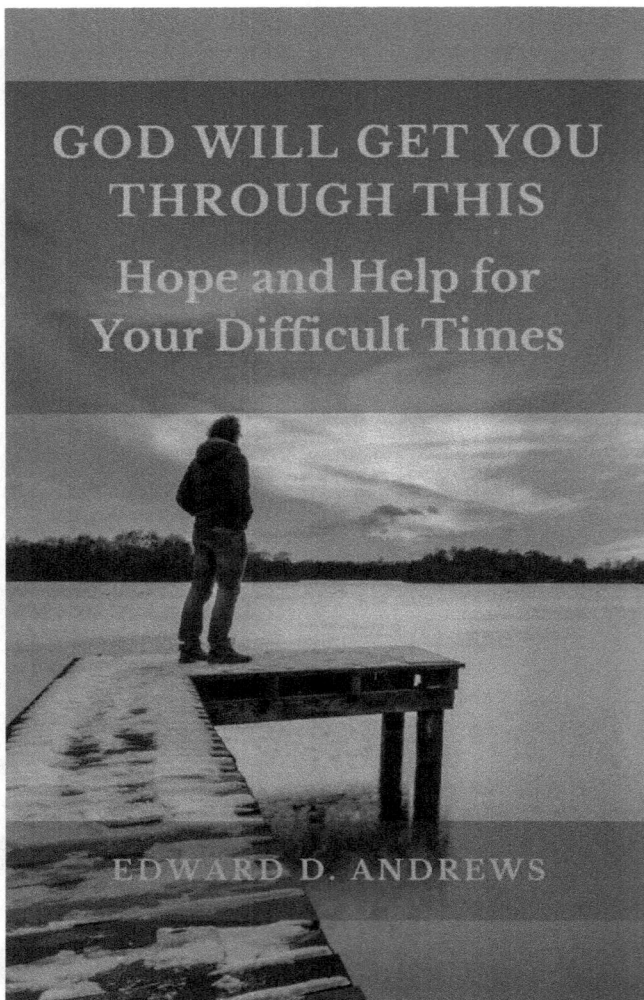

GOD WILL GET YOU THROUGH THIS

Hope and Help for Your Difficult Times

EDWARD D. ANDREWS

Christian Publishing House
ISBN-13: 978-1-945757-72-3

ISBN-10: 1-945757-72-8

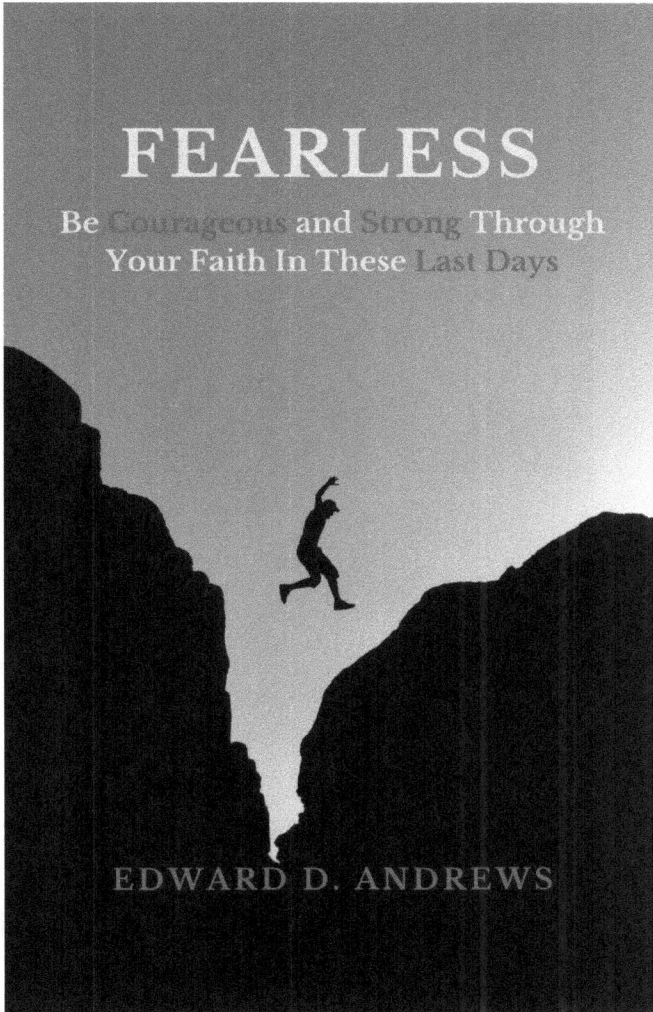

Christian Publishing House
ISBN-13: 978-1-945757-69-3

ISBN-10: 1-945757-69-8

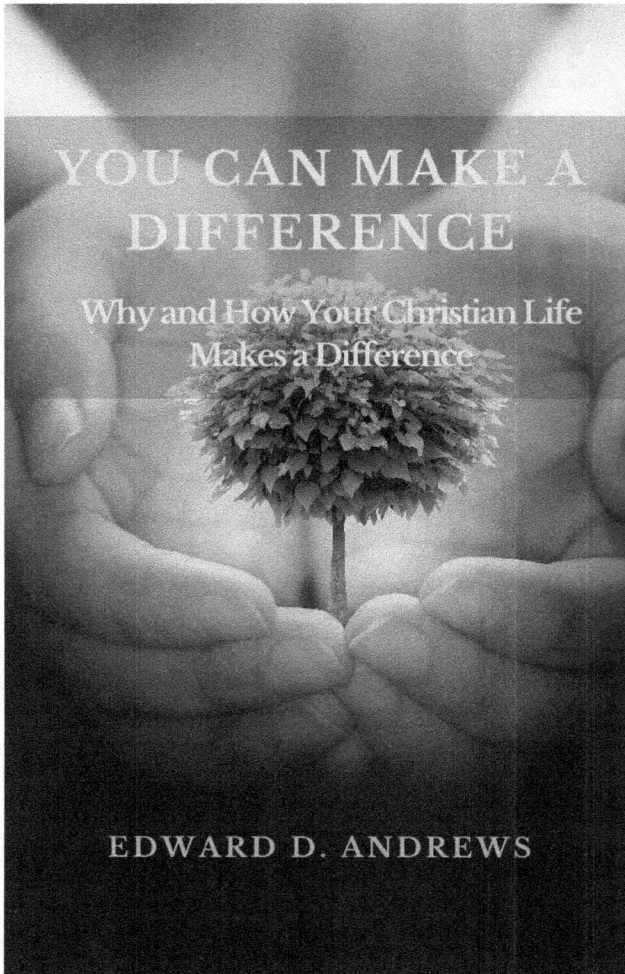

YOU CAN MAKE A DIFFERENCE

Why and How Your Christian Life Makes a Difference

EDWARD D. ANDREWS

Christian Publishing House

ISBN-13: 978-1-945757-74-7

ISBN-10: 1-945757-74-4

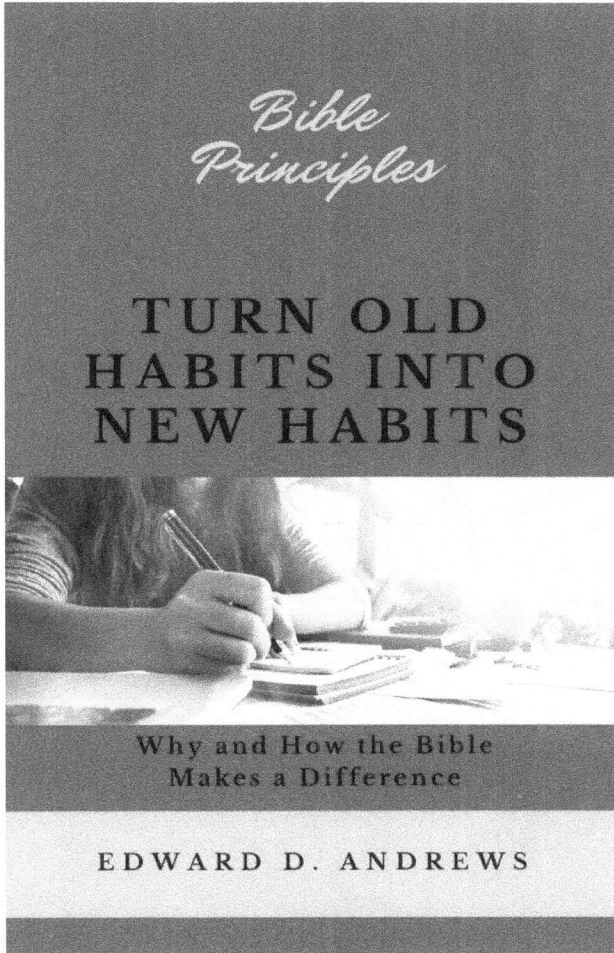

Bible Principles

TURN OLD HABITS INTO NEW HABITS

Why and How the Bible Makes a Difference

EDWARD D. ANDREWS

Christian Publishing House
ISBN-13: 978-1-945757-73-0

ISBN-10: 1-945757-73-6

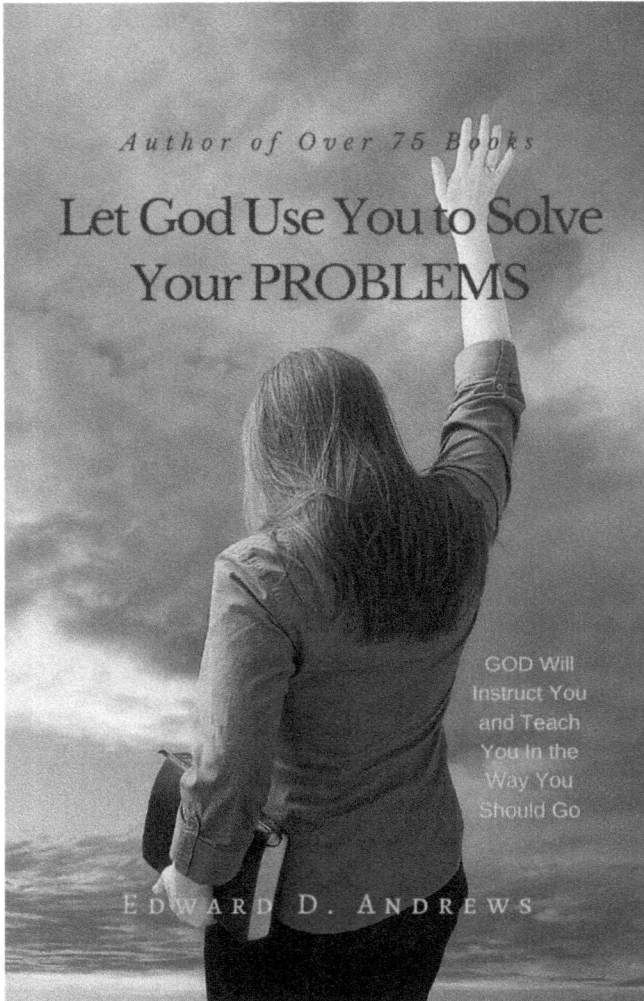

Author of Over 75 Books

Let God Use You to Solve Your PROBLEMS

GOD Will
Instruct You
and Teach
You In the
Way You
Should Go

EDWARD D. ANDREWS

Christian Publishing House
ISBN-13: 978-1-945757-86-0
ISBN-10: 1-945757-86-8

Author of Over 75 Books

PROMISES OF
GOD'S GUIDANCE

God Show Me Your Ways, Teach Me Your
Paths, Guide Me In Your Truth and Teach Me

EDWARD D. ANDREWS

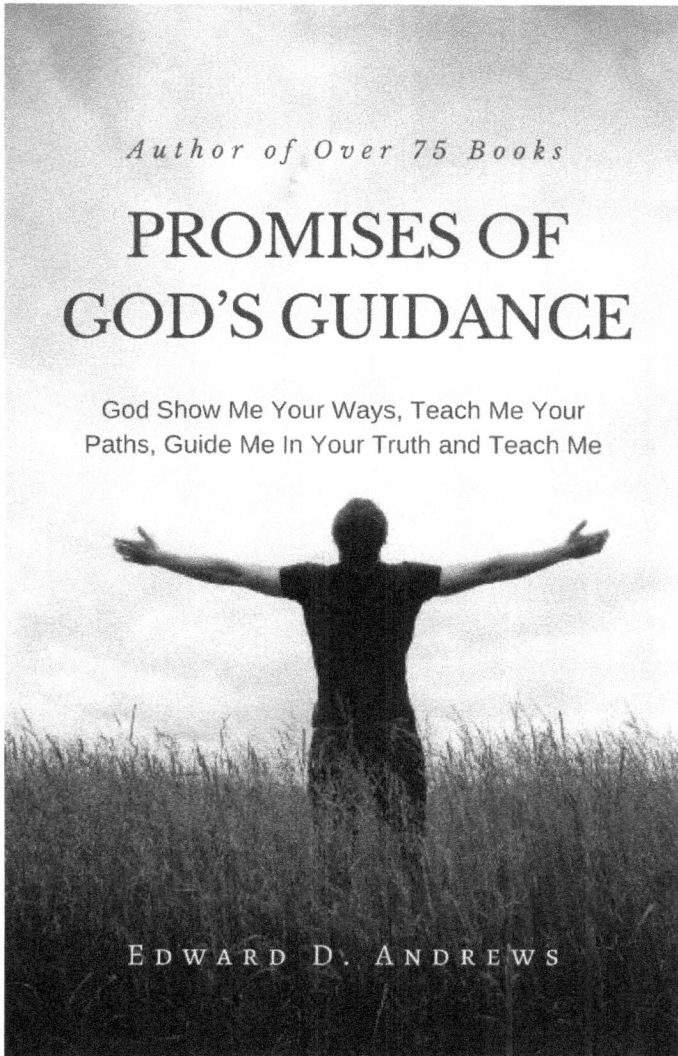

Christian Publishing House
ISBN-13: 978-1-945757-87-7

ISBN-10: 1-945757-87-6

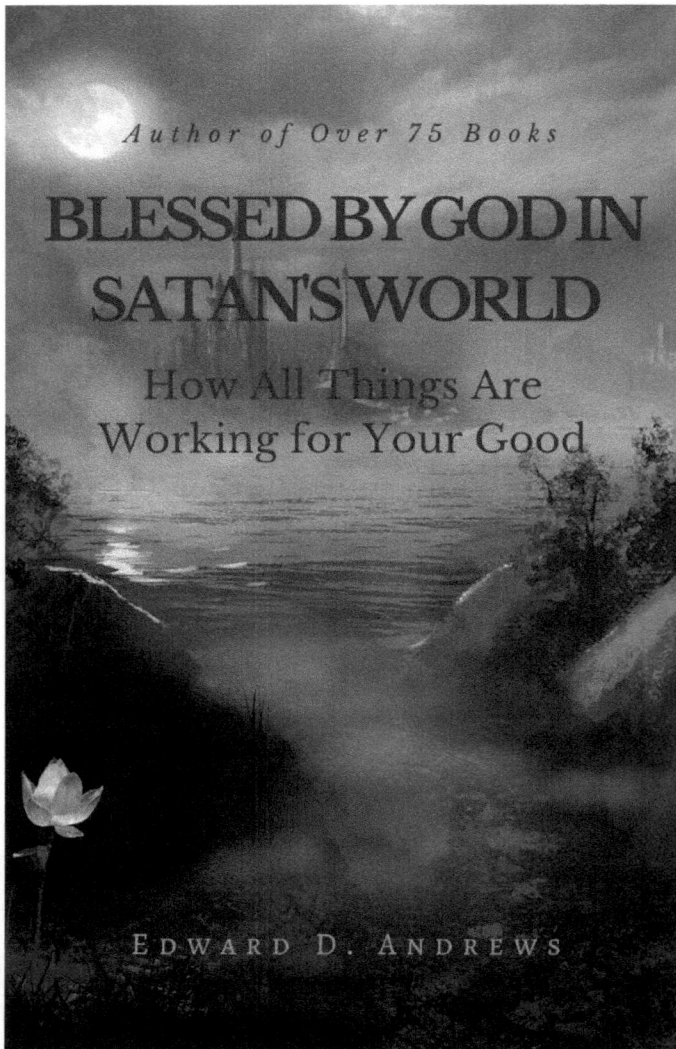

Author of Over 75 Books

BLESSED BY GOD IN SATAN'S WORLD

How All Things Are Working for Your Good

EDWARD D. ANDREWS

Christian Publishing House
ISBN-13: 978-1-945757-88-4

ISBN-10: 1-945757-88-4

HOW TO STUDY YOUR BIBLE

Rightly Handling the Word of God

Edward D. Andrews

Christian Publishing House
ISBN-13: 978-1-945757-62-4

ISBN-10: 1-945757-62-0

CHRISTIAN
APOLOGETIC EVANGELISM

REACHING HEARTS WITH THE ART OF PERSUASION

All Christians Are Scripturally Obligated to
Evangelize—Matt. 24:14; 28:19-20; Ac 1:8

EDWARD D. ANDREWS

Christian Publishing House
ISBN-13: 978-1-945757-75-4

ISBN-10: 1-945757-75-2

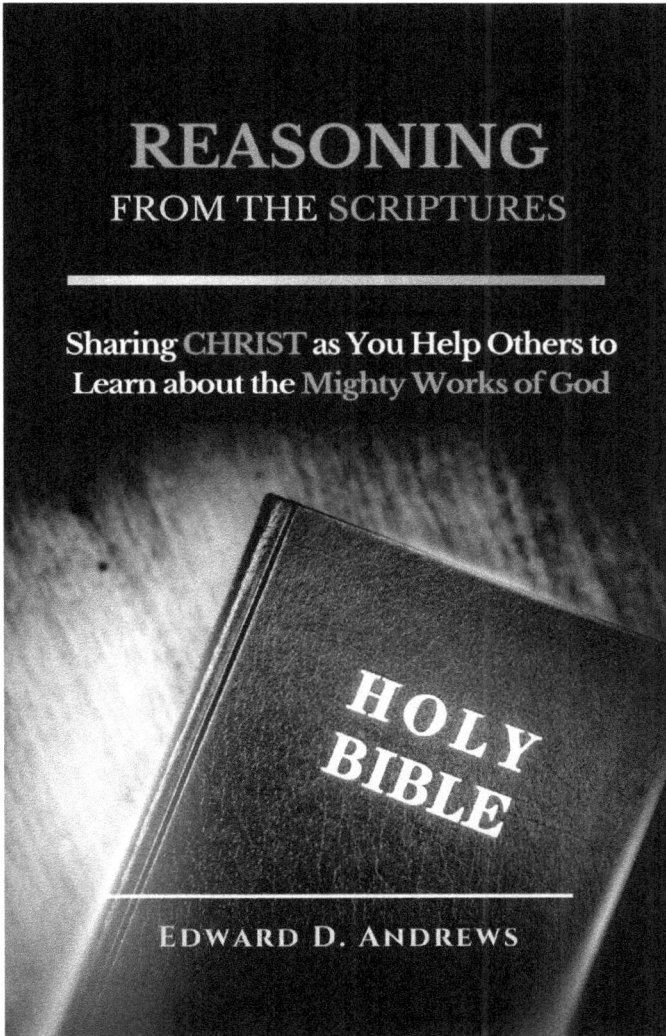

REASONING
FROM THE SCRIPTURES

Sharing CHRIST as You Help Others to
Learn about the Mighty Works of God

HOLY
BIBLE

EDWARD D. ANDREWS

Christian Publishing House
ISBN-13: 978-1-945757-82-2

ISBN-10: 1-945757-75-2

THE EMPATHY CHRONICLES

Rejoice With Those Who rejoice, Weep With Those Who Weep, and Suffer With Those Who Suffer

Terry Jamieson

Christian Publishing House

ISBN-13: 978-1-945757-35-8

ISBN-10: 1-945757-35-3

Foreword by Norman L. Geisler

JUDY SALISBURY

REASONS FOR FAITH

THE FIRST APOLOGETIC GUIDE FOR
CHRISTIAN WOMEN ON MATTERS OF THE
HEART, SOUL, AND MIND

Updated and Expanded Second Edition

Christian Publishing House
ISBN-13: 978-1-945757-43-3
ISBN-10: 1-945757-43-4